GOING
DEEPER

Foreword by Corey Russell

GOING DEEPER

40-Week Discipleship Guide
to Encountering Jesus

PART 2

JEFF MOOTZ

PRAYER DISCIPLESHIP
— PRESS —
Sioux Falls

GOING DEEPER

Published by Prayer Discipleship Press, Sioux Falls, SD.

First Edition: 2024
Going Deeper / Jeff Mootz
Paperback ISBN: 979-8-9898736-0-9
eBook ISBN: 979-8-9898736-1-6
Library of Congress Control Number: 2022904855

PRAYER DISCIPLESHIP
— PRESS —
Sioux Falls

GOING DEEPER
VIDEO COURSE

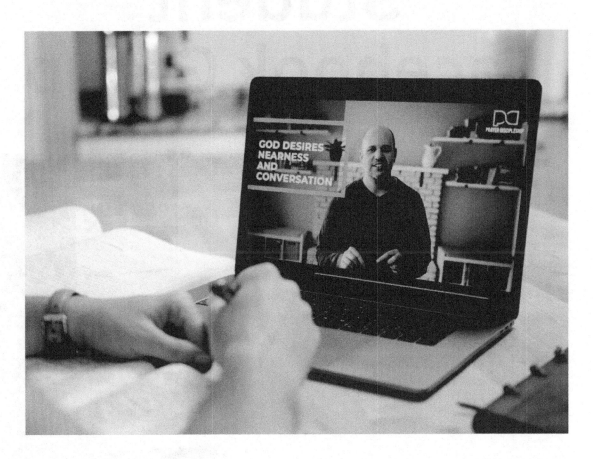

www.prayerdiscipleship.com

Read the book with the extra help of 80+ teaching and demonstration videos.

Join The Student Facebook Group

Request Access by emailing
support@prayerdiscipleship.com

DEDICATION

I dedicate this book to my joyful friends and staff who have helped launch and sustain the Underground Housee of Prayer and Encounter Church in Sioux Falls these past 10 years. God has heard every single whisper, groan, chorus, and prayer, and He's going to answer perfectly in His wise timing.

CONTENTS

Endorsements   *1*
Acknowledgments   *3*
Foreword   *5*

Module 5
Deliverance

Module Introduction   8
Assignment Overview   9
Spiritual Pursuits   10
20. Demonic Strongholds   **12**
Discipleship Meeting Guide   22
21. Deliverance Guide   **24**
Leaders Deliverance Guide   35
22. Walking Out Freedom: Prayer **39**
23. Walking Out Freedom: Church
Family   **46**

Module 6
Bible Study

Module Introduction   52
Assignment Overview   53
Spiritual Pursuits   55
24. Bible Study Approaches   **57**
Discipleship Meeting Guide   66
25. Book Study Part 1   **68**
26. Book Study Part 2   **77**
Discipleship Meeting Guide   88
27. Word Studies &
Interpretation   **90**
Discipleship Meeting Guide   100

Module 7
Throne Room

Module Introduction   104
Assignment Overview   105
Spiritual Pursuits   106
28. Seated in God's Temple   **108**
**29. God's Throne & Glorious
Colors**   **116**
Discipleship Meeting Guide   126
30. God's Glory Storm   **128**
31. Around God's Throne   **137**
Discipleship Meeting Guide   148

Module 8
Fasting

Module Introduction   152
Assignment Overview   153
Spiritual Pursuits   155
32. Lovesick Fasting   **157**
33. Weekly Fasting Part 1   **166**
Discipleship Meeting Guide   176
34. Weekly Fasting Part 2   **179**
35. Weekly Fasting Part 3   **184**
Discipleship Meeting Guide   194
36. Transition Week   **196**
Transition Assignment   200
Discipleship Meeting Guide   203

ENDORSEMENTS

I remember when I finally confessed that I didn't enjoy praying or the reading the Bible. My "devotions" were nothing more than a religious ritual. Then, a friend helped me realize that a season of discipline could launch me into a relationship with God that was actually enjoyable. It was so effective that I now teach this life-transforming message to thousands of people around the world. Jeff Mootz has now taken this same teaching and made it accessible to everyone. *Going Deeper* is a simple, hands on, and Biblical guide to the kind of enjoyable friendship with Jesus you have always wanted. It's time to turn duty into delight. This is your way forward. Don't delay!

Murray Hiebert
Director - OneEleven Global

Jeff Mootz has a rich history of personally loving Jesus and encountering Jesus' heart that has encouraged and provoked me over our 15 years of friendship. He has taken from that history and written one of the clearest, most inspiring books on encountering Jesus that I've ever read. *Going Deeper* is a clarion call to cultivating a lifestyle of encounter that many desire but few have clarity to intentionally pursue. Jeff does not stay in the theoretical, ethereal realm of vision alone—though does present a high vision of experiential encounters with God—but offers practical tools and discipleship structures to equip believers for breakthrough in their hearts and in their relationship with Jesus. This guided journey is a gift to the body of Christ globally that will play a pivotal role in preparing communities of believers to grow continually in love for Jesus until He returns.

Daniel Grenz
International Missionary – Firestarters Academy

It's hard for me to think of people who enjoy their relationship with God more than Jeff Mootz. Consequently, when he talks about discipleship and how to build a friendship with Jesus through disciplines like prayer, fasting and Bible study... I listen. I'm thrilled to have Jeff's book as a companion for my personal growth, but also excited to offer it as a helpful tool to our congregation as well.

David Sinkgraven
Senior Pastor: Life Church - Sioux Falls, South Dakota

As we get closer to the return of Jesus, the earth will experience great shaking and great revival. God is raising up a company of messengers who have invested the time to go deep in their relationship with Jesus to catch His heart, understand His Word, and proclaim His message with great authority. Jeff and Bethany Mootz are two of these messengers. They have invested years of their lives going deep with God and discipling a company of these messengers at the Underground House of Prayer in Sioux Falls, South Dakota. I highly recommend his book *Going Deeper* and encourage you to invest the time to gather a few friends and go through this 40-week journey together. The book is laid out in such a way that it will help you to develop lifestyle rhythms of prayer that will help you encounter God deeply, continually grow in your relationship with God, and bear much fruit for His glory!

Jeff Mann
Author of *Relentless Passion: Encounter God and burn with passion for Jesus* and *God's Eternal Plan for People and the Earth*

Jeff Mootz and the *Underground House of Prayer* have been a Godsend for our high school & middle school campus ministry. Jeff's calling to be an intercessor has blessed many people, and it has been a covering for the entire Sioux Falls region. I am personally grateful and know that this book will help people dive deeper into communication and fascination with our Savior. May Jesus fill you and burn a fire in your soul as you spend time praising Him and hearing Him speak to you.

John Glasser
Founder – Collision Ministry

ACKNOWLEDGMENTS

Thank you to my wife Bethany for non-stop encouragement, affirmation, ideas, editing, and strategy meetings about the content and flow of this curriculum. The substance of your personal life in God and your zeal for discipleship are all over these pages.

Thank you, Susan Blosser, for reading every single page of this book through every phase of writing. I could never repay you for all the hours of work you put in. Your daily encouragement and detailed corrections helped make the book what it is!

Thank you to my friends at Encounter Church (Jerry Mootz, Brandon and Tammy Smith, Bethany and Francis John, and Aubrey Anderson) who have tested this curriculum, given feedback, and labored to see people experience the beauty and love of Jesus.

Francis John, thank you for your encouragement and labors in setting up the online curriculum.

David Stokes, thank you for pouring over these pages in the editing process and bringing your expertise in writing and pastoring.

Mom and Dad, thank you for your overwhelming support, celebration of victories, and life-long display of what it looks like to love Jesus in every season. Dad, the greatest privilege a son could have is to minister and pray with a fiery dad every day of the week as his full-time occupation. Because of you, I have a long- term vision to be wholehearted, joyful, and to love my family.

FOREWORD

I've read many books on prayer, been to many conferences on prayer, and heard many messages on prayer, yet I've rarely been around many of the same people who actually pray. It's sad to say that there are few people whose very presence carries the fragrance of heaven on their life, whose words release power and conviction, and whose actions point to a living faith in God.

I've recently been struck by Jesus and His discipleship model in Luke 11. After spending 3 1/2 years with the Son of God, the disciples asked Jesus one thing: "Teach us to Pray." They watched Him pray, heard Him pray. They witnessed the countless times when He woke up early and withdrew into the wilderness and prayed. I believe this left the greatest impact on the disciples.

I've given my life to the place of prayer over the past 20 years, and there have only been a handful of people I've consistently witnessed who've stayed true to prayer, fasting, and ministry to God—Jeff Mootz is one of these few. He and his wife, Bethany, graduated from our Bible school at IHOP-KC and ran close with me during their last two years. Their faithfulness, humility, hunger, and purity constantly provoked me and called me higher in God.

Since 2014, Jeff and Bethany have taken the DNA and lifestyle of the house of prayer in Kansas City and established a praying church that hosts city-wide prayer hours a day. This book isn't simply good messages but has been tried and tested in doing it versus talking about it. They have walked through the failures, successes, victories, and setbacks involved in continually calling people to God.

Going Deeper is a prophetic call to the Body of Christ to connect with our original design for intimacy with God through daily prayer with brothers and sisters in community. Friend, you were made by God and for God, and you will never be satisfied until you live out of that fellowship with God. God longs for friendship and intimacy with you and He enjoys the process and journey of relating to you. Jeff calls us to push past the barriers of our culture and even our own souls into a deeper place of encounter with God and His heart. He also highlights the barriers that stand in the way and how we can practically get through them.

I wholeheartedly endorse this man and this message, and I am excited to see this material get out and touch this generation. Again, there are few people whose life of prayer is greater than the message they preach. Jeff Mootz is one of these people, and I pray that God multiplies him and this message across the earth.

–Corey Russell
Author and Speaker

MODULE 5

DELIVERANCE

MODULE INTRODUCTION

The purpose of this deliverance module is to equip you in understanding how to walk out freedom from sin and lie patterns as a long-term lifestyle. In this module, you will learn about demonic strongholds, how to identify and pray through them, and how to walk in spiritual freedom. For the next few weeks, your focus will be on praying through the patterns you've been talking about with your Discipleship Mentor. With a focused and well-rounded Biblical approach to freedom, levels of breakthrough can happen in every season. As a reminder, here are the four ways in which this discipleship program is set up to train you in a lifestyle of freedom:

1. **Encounter God** – Experiencing intimacy with God is the starting place for walking in freedom, and it's the way to maintain freedom long-term. Learning the prayer expressions positions you to encounter God.

2. **Intentional pursuit of freedom** – Sin and lie patterns are transformed the quickest when they are identified and addressed in a focused way. Orient your Bible pursuits (meditation, Bible study) around the truths you need to receive freedom.

3. **Accountability** – We have you meeting with a Discipleship Mentor to encourage you in your life in God and grow you in a lifestyle of accountability. Accountability relationships are a part of walking out freedom because they bring you out of hiddenness, shame, levels of passivity in pursuing God, and help to bring you into a greater sense of being fully known and celebrated by God and others.

4. **Deliverance prayer** – Receiving deliverance prayer is a major part of experiencing freedom from negative patterns, which is why it's the focus for an entire module. It is healthy to receive deliverance prayer in every season, and the more you do it, the more you'll be equipped to pray with others. Deliverance prayer supernaturally addresses demons and broken parts of the heart that are energizing darkness and hindering transformation.

ASSIGNMENT OVERVIEW
MODULE 5 – DELIVERANCE

For Weeks 23-25, schedule a 1 ½ - 2-hour deliverance prayer time in place of your weekly Discipleship Mentor meetings. These deliverance prayer times can be done with a local Sozo ministry (bethelsozo.com/sozo-network/) or with your Discipleship Mentor. Continue to follow your prayer schedule and Spiritual Pursuits each week.

Week Twenty-two Assignments:

- ❑ Read Chapter 20 – "**Demonic Strongholds.**" Journal your thoughts and questions about the chapter.
- ❑ Take one prayer time to identify strongholds God is highlighting in this season.
- ❑ Fill out a new *Spiritual Pursuits Document* for this module. Be intentional to add praying in tongues to your prayer schedule while maintaining your Bible reading, meditation, prayer list, and corporate prayer times.
- ❑ **Meet with your Discipleship Mentor.**

Week Twenty-three Assignments:

- ❑ Read Chapter 21 – "**Deliverance Guide.**" Journal your thoughts and questions about the chapter.
- ❑ **Meet with your Discipleship Mentor for a Deliverance Prayer Time.**

Week Twenty-four Assignments:

- ❑ Read Chapter 22 – "**Walking Out Freedom: Prayer.**" Journal your thoughts and questions about the chapter.
- ❑ Complete the forgiveness prayer time in one of your prayer times this week.
- ❑ **Meet with your Discipleship Mentor for a Deliverance Prayer Time.**

Week Twenty-five Assignments:

- ❑ Read Chapter 23 – "**Walking out Freedom: Church Family.**" Journal your thoughts and questions about the chapter.
- ❑ Answer the Church Family related questions.
- ❑ **Meet with your Discipleship Mentor for a Deliverance Prayer Time.**

SPIRITUAL PURSUITS   *DATE:* _____

1. **Bible reading direction and plan**
   (Write down what you will read and when you will read it):

2. **Meditation verse** (Choose a verse that speaks truth into your heart issue):

3. **Sin/character issue from which to get freedom:**

4. **Lie from which to pursue deliverance:**

5. **Gifting to pursue** (Include simple ways you can pursue it):

6. **Weekly Prayer Schedule**—Write down your plan for the *specific times* you are committed to spending with God each day, and *what specifically you plan to do during those times*. Include what your study or meditation focus will be. Refer to the example schedule in Chapter Two. (e.g., Monday 6-6:30 am—Tongues, 6:30-7:30 am—Meditation on Song of Solomon 1:2)

Monday

Tuesday

Wednesday

Thursday

Friday

Saturday

Sunday

20

DEMONIC STRONGHOLDS

JESUS WILL DELIVER YOU

The Spirit of the Lord God is upon Me, because the Lord has anointed Me to preach good tidings to the poor; He has sent Me to heal the brokenhearted, to proclaim liberty to the captives, and the opening of the prison to those who are bound.—Isaiah 61:1

Jesus is anointed to deliver those who are bound in sin and struggles. The Father sent Him to the earth to liberate us from the effects of sin and darkness, and He anointed Jesus with the full power of the Spirit to accomplish such a work. In fact, this is part of the gospel message. Jesus quoted Isaiah 61 the first time He identified Himself as the Messiah, which means that deliverance and freedom are core to Jesus' identity and the gospel message.[1]

Jesus' preaching of the kingdom was always accompanied by the works of the kingdom in healing and deliverance. He commissioned His followers to do the same, and they turned cities upside down as they cast out demons.[2] Casting out demons was synonymous with the preaching of the kingdom for Jesus and the early church because the gospel promises freedom from the kingdom of darkness. You can be confident that God will use others to help deliver you, and you will help deliver others by God's power.

---

[1] Luke 4:14-21.
[2] 2 Acts 5:16, 8:7, 16:18, 19:11.

Then His fame went throughout all Syria; and they brought to Him all sick people who were afflicted with various diseases and torments, and those who were demon-possessed, epileptics, and paralytics, and He healed them. —Matthew 4:24

Heal the sick, cleanse the lepers, raise the dead, cast out demons. Freely you have received, freely give. —Matthew 10:8

Jesus is the great liberator who destroys the work of the Devil![3] No demonic stronghold is too strong for Him, and no pattern is too deep or too long-term for Him.

JESUS IS ZEALOUS FOR YOUR FREEDOM

Jesus is zealous to set you free, and your freedom matters more to Him than it does to you. His eyes are on you, and His heart is filled with compassion towards your condition. God is not just waiting in heaven for you to figure things out by yourself—He's your Husband, and Father. Jesus is in the trenches with you, and He's fully involved in your issues at the deepest level. Trust that He's taking the initiative to bring you into freedom in each season.

Jesus is a jealous Bridegroom who wants every part of your heart freed up so that you can receive His affections and give Him all of yours. He's been weakening the walls of lies in your heart as you've been growing in friendship with Him these past few months, and now He wants to tear down the walls through deliverance. If you have felt unbelief around your deliverance or frustration over failed attempts to get free, break your agreement with unbelief out loud today, and renew your hope in Jesus' desire and power to deliver you.

---

[3] 1 John 3:8.

INTRODUCTION TO SPIRITUAL STRONGHOLDS

For the weapons of our warfare are not carnal but mighty in God for pulling down strongholds, casting down arguments and every high thing that exalts itself against the knowledge of God, bringing every thought into captivity to the obedience of Christ.—2 Corinthians 10:4-5

In the natural, strongholds are fortresses or castles protected by thick and tall walls to keep out enemies. In the spiritual, strongholds are places in the soul and body where walls are built up to protect something. These strongholds are godly if they are walls of truth and righteousness, or these strongholds are demonically influenced if they are walls of sin and lies.

GODLY STRONGHOLDS

Godly strongholds are built up brick by brick by meditating on the Bible and making righteous decisions day after day. As we grow in agreement with God's values and truths, godly strongholds are made stronger and become harder for the enemy to penetrate with lies or temptations. These strongholds create places in our minds and hearts for God to manifest and dwell in a greater experiential way.[4] God came to live in our spirit-man the day we gave our lives to Him, but He inhabits places in our minds and hearts when we grow in agreement with truth and righteousness over time.

DEMONIC STRONGHOLDS

"Be angry, and do not sin": Do not let the sun go down on your wrath, nor give place to the devil.—Ephesians 4:26-27

When an unclean spirit goes out of a man, he goes through dry places, seeking rest and finds none.—Matthew 12:43

---

[4] John 14:21, 23; Ephesians 3:17.

Demonic strongholds are built up by agreeing with sin and lies day after day. In reality, a stronghold can begin with agreeing with a lie or participating in a sin a few times. From there, it can build on itself into something larger. If we grow in agreement with a sin or a lie, we allow that stronghold to get taller and stronger. Agreement with darkness gives legal access to demons to dwell in those places of the heart and mind and demonically energize sins and lies. Demonic strongholds create supernatural barriers that block the truth from truly entering the heart, and they darken thoughts and emotions. Demons are looking for places to live, and they want to destroy people, so they do everything in their power to create strongholds or homes for themselves in humans.[5] In Ephesians 4, Paul warned believers not to "give place" to the devil, which meant legal access to their hearts.

If God perhaps will grant them repentance, so that they may know the truth, and that they may come to their senses and escape the snare of the devil, having been taken captive by him to do his will.—2 Timothy 2:25-26

Demonic strongholds are torn down brick by brick by agreeing with God through confession, repentance, forgiveness, and Biblical meditation. These spiritual means are a huge part of "renewing the spirit of our minds."[6] Deliverance prayer times help tear down bricks because they are focused on agreeing with God and breaking agreement with lies and sins through confession and repentance.

ADDRESSING DEMONS IS NECESSARY

As they went out, behold, they brought to Him a man, mute and demon-possessed. And when the demon was cast out, the mute spoke.—Matthew 9:32-33

Then they came to Jesus, and saw the one who had been demon-possessed and had the legion, sitting and clothed and in his right mind. And they were afraid.—Mark 5:15

---

[5] Ephesians 4:23.

[6] ibid.

To get victory over demonic strongholds, you must deal with the stronghold and the demon behind any lie or sin pattern through repentance, forgiveness, and agreement with truth. Though not all the time, demons can block or be the source of physical, emotional, or mental illnesses.[7] Therefore, spiritual hindrances must be addressed in spiritual ways. Because of this principle, self-help methods and counseling methods that don't include the spiritual methods aren't very effective. The world's solutions to human problems can't offer deep freedom through non-spiritual means. There must be a spiritual transaction (repentance, forgiveness, casting out demons, agreement with truth) with Him to deal with a pattern that is rooted in spiritual things. Demons don't leave until the stronghold is torn down, and ungodly patterns don't stop until the demon is cast out, so why not pursue a method that addresses the root cause?

SPIRIT, SOUL, AND BODY

May your whole spirit, soul, and body be preserved blameless at the coming of our Lord Jesus Christ.—1 Thessalonians 5:23

For the flesh lusts against the Spirit, and the Spirit against the flesh; and these are contrary to one another, so that you do not do the things that you wish.—Galatians 5:17

Christians can have demonic strongholds in their souls (thoughts, emotions, will) and physical bodies (physical appetites and physical health) but not in their spirit-man.[8] Some people don't believe that Christians can have a demonic presence in them because they believe that the Holy Spirit completely possesses them after salvation. After salvation, the Holy Spirit resurrects our spirit-man and then lives in him. But our souls and bodies are not changed at salvation; the Holy Spirit progressively renews them as we participate with God in growing in revelation and character, which is called sanctification.

Our bodies have supernatural access to the Holy Spirit's life for divine healing and conquering physical lusts and urges. However, the fullness of salvation will not come

---

[7] Luke 13:10-16; Mark 9:17; Matthew 9:33, 12:22.
[8] Romans 7:23; James 1:14-15.

to our bodies until we receive our glorified bodies at Jesus' return.[9] A common way of communicating this principle is that our spirits are saved, our souls are being saved, and our bodies will be saved.

> *But if you have bitter envy and self-seeking in your hearts, do not boast and lie against the truth. This wisdom does not descend from above, but is earthly, sensual, demonic. For where envy and self-seeking exist, confusion and every evil thing are there.*—James 3:14-16

Our souls and bodies are open to demonic influence and strongholds because of our salvation's progressive and future nature. This means that you can still engage with lies or sins and open doors to demonic influence even after being a Christian. Therefore, you need Jesus to heal and deliver you from past lies and sins and any demonic strongholds that have been created because of demonic influence.

LEVELS OF DEMONIC INFLUENCE

There are varying levels of demonic influence within the category of demonic strongholds. These levels are important to understand and identify so that you can deal with strongholds properly. Understanding the idea that there are levels of demonic influence also removes the idea that someone with a demon is automatically fully possessed by a demon.

LEVEL #1 – ATTACK/ACCUSATION

Every believer has to resist momentary accusations or temptations from the demonic realm at times. This shouldn't be a constant reality throughout the day.

The amount that it happens and the amount that it moves us depends on our spiritual maturity in Christ. Satan accuses the church night and day to get us to agree with his lies so that demons can build strongholds.[10] The enemy can also attack by causing circumstances to flare up, stirring up relational conflict (usually through accusation),

---

[9] Romans 8:23.

[10] Revelation 12:10.

releasing physical heaviness, tempting us to lust, and stirring up our emotions in a heightened way. As believers, we're called to resist and quench these "fiery darts of the wicked one."[11]

LEVEL #2 – OPPRESSION

In my opinion, there are many levels of oppression, and most deliverance needs would fall into this category. I believe most Christians have some level of oppression they could address. Oppression is a heightened measure of demonic influence that is consistently experienced in specific areas (thoughts, emotions, behavior, physical symptoms) due to spiritual strongholds. We still choose to think, feel, and do negative things out of our free will, but the enemy adds supernatural energy to those areas in the moment and helps to keep us in ungodly cycles.

Oppression is different from attack because there is some level of agreement at the heart level with the lies or accusations, and it manifests in the way a person behaves or thinks. An oppressed person experiences the same temptations with heightened urges and accusations (or overwhelming negative emotions) that seem hard to break out of on a near-daily basis. In these moments, they almost always give way to them. Example temptations, accusations, and overwhelming emotions could be fear, rejection, shame, loneliness, confusion, anxiety, bitterness, levels of panic attack, anger, addictions, and lustful or perverted sexual desires.

LEVEL #3 – HINDERED

This level of demonic influence is a severe level of demonic influence and is stronger and more consistent than the oppression levels. People in this category feel tormented by dark thoughts, heavy emotions, or perverted desires. They also struggle to spend time with God due to experiencing intense accusation in their hearts and feel powerless in battling a sin or lie and have little to no hope to overcome it. People in this category find it hard to sustain normal living because they are severely "hindered" in one ore more ways.

LEVEL #4 – DOMINATION (POSSESSION)

Christians cannot be dominated by or possessed by a demon because it requires a very deep level of agreement. Domination means that the demon has an extremely high level of

---

[11] Ephesians 6:16; 2 Corinthians 12:7.

control over a person. Some people use the term "domination" instead of possession because it communicates the feeling of being overwhelmed by a demon while still having a free will. It is common for Christians who are newer to the deliverance topic to assume everyone with a demonic stronghold is possessed, but this isn't the case, and it leads to many misunderstandings and unnecessary fears.[12]

DISCERNING STRONGHOLDS

#1 - OBSERVE PATTERNS

There are several ways to determine if you have some level of a stronghold in your life. The first way is to take an honest look at your life and write down any lies, negative emotions, or sins that you struggle with on a daily or weekly basis. What lies do you struggle with consistently? What triggers you into an emotional swirl, and when does it usually happen? What sin do you act out consistently?

Let the following physical description help you identify strongholds that you may not be aware of. My dad uses the language of "emotional bruises" when talking about identifying personal strongholds. Physical bruises are very sensitive to the touch, and they hurt a lot if someone bumps into them. The level of pain associated with being bumped by someone doesn't make sense in the moment, but it makes sense if you understand that there is trauma deep in your tissue. Emotional bruises are similar in that they're caused by something in your past and create a deep wound that needs healing. That past wound can be "bumped" by people or circumstances around you and cause an illogical amount of emotional pain. The emotional pain or swirl of accusation isn't necessarily the fault of the person or the circumstance in front of you; it's the result of the past wound that wasn't healed.

You can also ask close family and friends what they see in your life. You may not identify some patterns because they have become normal to you, but others have an outside and possibly clearer perspective than you do, which can be helpful. They can see your sins towards others or themselves, see unhealthy patterns of living, and they can hear you speak out lies that you believe. Going back to the bruise analogy, you naturally

---

[12] Matthew 17:14-18; Luke 4:33-35, 8:27-33.

protect your emotional bruises from being "hit by others or circumstances" by arranging or orienting your life in certain ways. Those around you might be able to see your bruises and how you're protecting them.

#2 – ASK GOD

The second way to discern strongholds is to take a prayer time to ask the Holy Spirit if you have a stronghold. He will bring a word to mind, an image, or an overall awareness of an issue with memories of when you fall into the pattern. Ask the Holy Spirit questions about what He brings to mind to get further clarity on the heart issue.

#3 – EXAMPLE STRONGHOLDS

The third way to discern a possible stronghold is to review a list like the one below to see if you identify with any of them. If you know you struggle with something on this list, take time to ask God for clarity about how and when it affects you. Here is an example stronghold list:

1. Fear
2. Anxiety (stress, worry, panic attacks)
3. Passivity/laziness
4. Unbelief
5. Unforgiveness/bitterness
6. Legalism
7. Control/manipulation
8. Pride/arrogance
9. Self-hatred (personality, gifting, body)
10. Anger
11. Rejection
12. Abandonment/orphan spirit
13. Sexual perversion (past or current pattern)
14. Occult practice/witchcraft/drug use
15. Traumas

EVIDENCE OF BROKEN STRONGHOLDS

When a stronghold is addressed, and any level of demonic influence is removed, some immediate fruits are clarity of mind, increased godly desires (worship, righteousness), a sense of intimacy with God, and the ability to identify and resist old patterns. Strongholds and demons are supernatural and have a real impact on the human heart, so when they're broken, there should be a supernatural relief from the darkness and an increase of God's felt presence. I say this to help you realize that you're in a spiritual battle, to give you

I see these fruits in those I lead through deliverance prayer, but I've also experienced them myself when I've received prayer. In my first deliverance prayer time, I received freedom from a spirit of anger. As I asked God to highlight an issue to address, He brought the word "anger" to mind three times, so my friends and I asked Him to reveal the root sins or memories connected to anger. Each time He brought up a memory of me acting out in anger, I repented and felt something loosening from my heart. As I repented of the last memory and rebuked the demon, I felt something lift off me and felt an increased peace and God's presence come upon me. After that day, I was better able to recognize the past anger patterns and resist them. I was more patient, and I felt more empowered to resist or healthily process anger when it arose instead of it overtaking me.

In another scenario, I prayed for a person who was addicted to drugs, alcohol, and cigarettes who experienced these same fruits after prayer. In our prayer time, God highlighted trauma and unforgiveness as sources of his addictions. As he forgave each person by name and repented of believing specific lies, we all felt darkness leave and God's presence come. The person felt such a release that he sat for several minutes breathing in peace and then laughing in joy. At the end, he began to weep and praise Jesus out of gratitude. As a fruit of addressing strongholds and demonic influence, this person never struggled with his addictions again in the four years that I knew him. He even went on to go through Bible school and thrive in the midst of hard life circumstances.

These supernatural moments are your portion, too. God is near you, and He has the supernatural power to deliver you from any issue you've struggled with. He's overseeing your deliverance, and He wants all your heart freed up to receive His love and give Him your love.

WEEKLY ASSIGNMENT

Take at least 30 minutes in a prayer time this week to ask God for clarity in identifying which strongholds He's wanting you to address right now. Using the three suggested ways to identifying strongholds in the chapter, write down your own observations of broken patterns in your life. Write down the thoughts, images, memories, and emotions God brings to mind. Also, ask God about the heart issue you've been praying about and discussing since the beginning of the program. What you sense from the Lord in this prayer time will be the prayer agenda for your deliverance prayer sessions throughout this module.

DISCIPLESHIP MEETING GUIDE
MODULE 5: DELIVERANCE – CHAPTER 20

MEETING FOCUS:

The purpose of this meeting is to discuss the topic of spiritual strongholds and prepare for the deliverance prayer sessions of this module.

DISCUSSION QUESTIONS (IN ORDER OF IMPORTANCE):

1. *Chapter Questions:*
   a. Chapter 20 – Discuss any journaled thoughts and questions from the chapter.
   b. Identifying Strongholds assignment - In-depth, share how your prayer time went and what you sensed God revealing to you about your strongholds. We will focus praying through these strongholds in the deliverance prayer times this month.
2. *Spiritual Pursuits:*
   a. Practically, how is your prayer schedule going? How many days have you walked out your prayer schedule? How are your Bible study, meditation, prayer list, and tongues times going, and how is God impacting you through them?
   b. Briefly review your new *Spiritual Pursuits Document.*
3. Briefly review next week's homework together. Decide when your first deliverance session will be and what needs to be done before in preparation for it.

MEETING NOTES:

_____

_____

_____

_____

_____

_____

_____

_____

_____

_____

21

DELIVERANCE GUIDE

(WRITTEN BY BETHANY MOOTZ)

▋ INTRODUCTION

This chapter is a practical guide to praying through strongholds with a Biblical approach (confession, repentance, and forgiveness). The practical steps and values are very similar to most inner-healing and deliverance models. After reading it, you should understand the basic flow of what a prayer time can look like, how God will speak, and how you can respond to His leading. More training and experience will always be helpful, but the simple truths of this guide are substantial enough to equip you to begin receiving and facilitating basic prayer times. These tools are designed to be used with one or two people praying over another person, but they will also help you pray through strongholds in your own prayer times moving forward.

As you read through what a deliverance prayer time can look like and consider your own deliverance sessions in this module, understand that they are intimate and presence-filled times with Jesus. You will encounter the Psalm 139 God who, in delight and desire, searches and knows your every detail and reveals His thoughts towards you in the smallest of moments of your past. Jesus never brings fear, shame, or condemnation in these prayer times. He only brings clarity, love, comfort, and forgiveness.

SPIRITUAL OPEN DOORS

Let us lay aside every weight, and the sin which so easily ensnares us, and let us run with endurance the race that is set before us, looking unto Jesus, the author and finisher of our faith, who for the joy that was set before Him endured the cross.—Hebrews 12: 1-2

Through the grace of the cross, Jesus has forgiven and empowered you to run your spiritual race. Running your grace-empowered race includes choosing to lay aside everything that hinders you. Hebrews 12 says to throw off "weights" and "snares." Sins ensnare and are open doors to darkness. Weights are lifestyle choices, emotional wounds, or anything that weighs you down while running your race. What areas of your life do you need to lay aside or throw off so that you can run with endurance and joy?

Open doors give the demonic kingdom legal permission to influence us and occur when we agree with darkness or have in the past. Once opened, the enemy works to grow them into strongholds. Open doors remain open to the enemy's influence until we actively shut them through spiritual means.

Identifying open doors isn't a "witch hunt" or a systematic figuring out of the names of demons you might have. Instead, it can be a lifestyle where it's a delight to ask God what hindrances He wants to highlight and free us from. It's an intimate conversation with Jesus our Bridegroom to bring forth greater freedom and love.

THREE OPEN DOORS TO DARKNESS

When you seek the Holy Spirit for clarity in your prayer times, there are three common areas that He will highlight to you as open doors to darkness.[1] Even though the open doors overlap, separating them helps deal with each open door in Biblical ways.

1. **Sins** you commit – unforgiveness/anger, involvement in sexual sins, occult (innocent or purposeful), viewing or listening to sinful entertainment, lying, covetousness, jealousy, anger, drunkenness, drug use, etc.

---

[1] Shelley Hundley, "Simplified Ministry Training—Praying for Deliverance and Healings," (Lecture Notes, International House of Prayer University, November 22, 2009).

2. **Injustices** against you – physical, sexual, and emotional abuse, differing levels of emotional trauma, rejection, betrayal, etc. Injustices could also include things that were not done for you.

3. **Lies** you have agreed with – things people have told you, things you have believed on your own because of your circumstances or the worldly culture (rejection, abandonment, fears, self-hatred, etc.)

BIBLICAL RESPONSES TO OPEN DOORS

1. **Sins** you commit – respond by ***confessing the sin*** out loud and acknowledging it as a sin. ***Repent of the sin*** by praying out loud that you choose to turn away from the sin and war against it in God's grace. ***Ask for forgiveness*** from God.

2. **Injustices** against you – respond by ***forgiving others, God, and yourself.***

3. **Lies** you believe – respond by ***breaking agreement with each lie***. Pray out loud that you reject the lies. Then break agreement with each lie specifically.

GOD'S CLEANSING TOUCH

As you respond to what God highlights, He responds to you! After you have confessed and received forgiveness in the prayer time, it's important to seek healing and cleansing from God for each open door. He wants to remove the darkness from your heart and replace it with truth, light, and His love. Expect to feel God's presence on your body and emotions as He washes the effects of sin and pain away. After prayer, your thoughts and emotions should feel freer and more peaceful because spiritual defilement will have been washed away. Defilement is a spiritual residue of darkness from sin and lies that rests on us and affects our thoughts and emotions until God washes it away.[2]

1. **Sins** you commit – He comes to cleanse you of defilement and forgive you. After confession, there is usually a feeling of being cleansed, forgiven, and embraced by God. ***Receive His forgiveness for your sins***.

2. **Injustices** against you – He comes to cleanse, bring comfort, remove pain, release inner healing, and restore what was stolen. After forgiving, there is usually a sense

---

[2] Matthew 15:11-20; 1 Corinthians 3:17; 8:17; Hebrews 12:15; James 3:6; Revelation 3:4.

of hope and peace and a sense that God is with you. There can also be a sense of emotional relief as pain is released to God. ***Picture Him washing you and removing your pain.***

3. **Lies** you believe – He comes to cleanse you and build a stronghold of truth. While praying to hear His truth, you will hear God whisper His perspective over you and feel His heart towards you. ***Give God time to speak His truth over you, and write down whatever He speaks.***

SIMPLE DELIVERANCE MODEL

Before you begin your prayer time, pray and command every demon to submit to the Lordship of Jesus, "In the name of Jesus, we command every demon to submit to Jesus. We say that you will not manifest in this room or in our hearts in any way." Before you begin a deliverance time with others, remind everyone that demons should not talk or manifest in any way. If there is a demonic manifestation (fear, anxiety, shaking, nausea, sleepiness, confusion) during the time, stop and command every demon to submit to Jesus.

STEP #1 - ASK

Identify the symptom that you or someone you are praying with is dealing with. This can be done before or during the prayer session using the steps from the previous chapter. It's like going to the doctor; what are your symptoms, and what do you need freedom from (fear, anxiety, addictions, pornography, anger, etc.)? Take a few minutes to ask the Lord what issue He's highlighting. God will bring a thought or picture to mind communicating what you need to pray about. Other times He may communicate through an inner knowing, which is like a "gut feeling." Or you can begin with the clearest negative symptom you are aware of in your life.

STEP #2 - REVEAL

Alone or together, ask God to highlight any of the three open doors (sins, injustices, or lies) that are connected to the symptom you've identified. In detail, write down what you sense God highlighting. Take your time during the entire process. God could highlight a memory of a clear injustice, lie, or sin, or it could be a thought that seems random. I've learned that the first few thoughts are most likely God talking, even if it doesn't make sense initially.

In this highlighting time, ask the Lord to reveal the root memory or the first time you agreed with your specific issue, not necessarily all the times you've acted out in the particular issue. For example, if you deal with anger, you don't necessarily have to address it every time you've been angry. In a deliverance time, God will highlight the memories where the pattern of anger began (example: acting out in anger or injustice that caused anger) and where the spirit of anger was first given legal access.

STEP #3 – REPENT

Respond to each open door God highlights by slowly praying through them one at a time. We must break agreement (repent) and resist the enemy and then respond to what God highlights **by speaking these out loud:**

1. **Sins** you commit – respond by *confessing the sin* out loud and acknow- ledging it as a sin. *Repent of the sin* by praying out loud that you choose to turn away from it and war against it in God's grace. *Ask for forgiveness* from God.
2. **Injustices** against you – respond by *forgiving others, God, and yourself.*
3. **Lies** you believe – respond by *breaking agreement with each lie.* Pray out loud that you reject the lies and then break agreement with each lie specifically.

STEP #4 – PROPHESY TRUTH

This step always includes a cleansing from defilement and pain. The open door might be closed, but now it's time to receive His forgiveness and comfort. Now's the time to let Him come into your emotional pain, bring inner healing, and let Him speak His truth over you. He does this because He wants to begin building strongholds of truth in place of the torn down demonic strongholds.

The way to receive the truth is to ask God for His perspective about the memory you just prayed through. In these memories and hurts, ask God where He was, how He felt, and what He was doing and saying to you. Allow Him space to prophesy truth over you. Usually, it's best for the person receiving prayer to hear God and share it before the prayer leader shares what God speaks to him or her.

For example, after praying through a time in my life where I felt rejected, in my imagination I took time to watch Jesus come into the negative memory and show me where He was. It was like I was a little girl again, and I saw Him looking at me with love and holding me at that moment. He was completely and thoughtfully engaged and singing over me! The real memory's emotions were the exact opposite of this, but after I broke agreement with the lies and shut the open doors, I felt His love being deposited into that memory. I felt accepted, and I felt restored in my emotions.

If there isn't a tangible emotional feeling of love, peace, or joy from God, or if you don't feel Him speaking quite yet, go back to Step 2 and Step 3. Tangible experiences almost always happen when God has done a full work, so there could be more memories that need to be highlighted and prayed through. If the scheduled session doesn't give time for this, have the prayer session recipient go back through steps 2 and 3 by themselves and then schedule another deliverance session. It is normal to need multiple prayer sessions.

STEP #5 – REBUKE

After praying through each door (repenting and prophesying truth), take time to command every demon connected to the sin and lie patterns to leave the individual. Empower them to speak a prayer like this out loud, "In Jesus name, I command every demon connected to these lies and sins to leave my life. I close all spiritual doors, and I say no to these lies and sin patterns." I encourage you to speak this out at a normal volume and not to hype up the moment. Your authority to cast out demons comes from Jesus' Kingship, not the loudness of your voice. Rebuking in a calm way magnifies Jesus' authority, diminishes the perception of demonic control, and teaches all those involved in the prayer time how to be supernaturally natural.

Rebuke after all doors are closed – Rebuking demons should only be done after you have responded to all the things God highlights pertaining to the one issue you're praying about. When it seems like God has stopped highlighting things, and the person receiving prayer has been feeling freedom in the prayer time, rebuke the demon. It's possible that demons leave when things are repented of, but it's still good to rebuke them out loud at the end. Demons must leave when all the legal doors have been closed and are commanded to leave the property. If there are still legal doors to close, the demons have a legal right to stay, so casting them out too early will be less effective.

What it feels like – When a demon is cast out, there should not be any demonic manifestations (shaking, vomiting, coughing, nausea, choking, fear). This is a helpful expectation to communicate to the person receiving prayer so that they are not worried about or waiting for a demonic manifestation as a sign of deliverance. If there is a demonic manifestation at any point in the deliverance process, stop and command every demon to submit to Jesus. When demons leave, there will usually be an obvious experience of God's presence, a feeling of heaviness or cloudiness lifting off the person, and a feeling of emotional and mental peace and stillness. It is even common for people to cry or praise Jesus out of relief and gratitude.

FORGIVENESS

Forgiveness is a very important part of pursuing freedom because so many dark things are wrapped up in unforgiveness or are the fruit of unforgiveness (bitterness, anger, control). When forgiveness is released, the foundations of demonic strongholds crumble and emotions become free. It is so simple but so powerful in deliverance prayer times.

First of all, forgiveness is a command from Jesus, not an option.[3] His eternal nature is to forgive, and the foundation of the gospel message is forgiveness. He delights in showing mercy and forgiving thousands of times, and He wants us to be like Him and experience the freedom of being merciful.[4] Everything that you have done to others or others have done to you can be forgiven.

Forgiveness is an acknowledgment of wrong things that have been to you.[5] When God highlights an issue to forgive in your prayer times, you should not minimize or dismiss it. Pray something like this, "Father, I acknowledge that this person wronged me (say what they did) and that it affected me." Forgiveness is also entrusting God to release justice to the person that wronged you and to the broken situation in His timing.[6] This releases your right to bring vengeance or collect the practical or emotional "debt" that is owed you.

Forgiveness allows for pain, anger, and other things to be released to God so He can fill your heart with His life. Pray something like this, "Father, I entrust You to judge this person and this situation in Your timing and in Your way. I release all rights to bring vengeance upon this person and this situation, and I release all the pain and anger to You. I completely forgive them for their debt to me."

---

[3] Mark 11:25-26.

[4] Matthew 18:21-22; Micah 7:18.

[5] R.T. Kendall, *Total Forgiveness—Revised and Updated*, (Lake Mary, FL: Charisma House, 2007), 23-24.

[6] Romans 12:19.

For more severe situations, forgiveness does not mean that you have to be friends with someone who's hurt you.[7] Once you have forgiven, you will be able to set godly boundaries with those who have hurt you and still aren't safe. In certain situations, this takes time to figure out with the counsel of others outside the situation. In God's healing power, you will grow in compassion for them and pray for them without having to relate with them.

CONFESSION

Confess your trespasses to one another, and pray for one another, that you may be healed.—James 5:16

If we confess our sins, He is faithful and just to forgive us our sins and to cleanse us from all unrighteousness.—1 John 1:9

Similar to forgiveness, confession and repentance are important parts of pursuing freedom. Confession and repentance are God's ordained way of restoring fellowship with Him, closing spiritual doors to darkness, and removing spiritual defilement. It's important to understand what these are and how to pray them during your deliverance sessions. This is also helpful in your daily walk with God.

Confession is acknowledging and taking responsibility for personal sin before God in order to restore fellowship with Him. Our sins don't cut us off from our relationship with God, and our confession doesn't earn right relationship with God. However, they do restore intimate fellowship with God. Like any human relationship where there's been sin, confession brings healing by acknowledging the relational hurt and dealing with it. When you sin, you're in disagreement with God. When you confess sin, you come back into agreement with God and can relate to Him with an open heart.

An overall legal forgiveness was applied to your life by the blood of Jesus at your salvation experience, but small relational forgiveness throughout your life between you and God is applied when you confess to Him. When confession happens, God washes away the spiritual defilement that rested on your thoughts and emotions as a result of your

---

[7] Ibid., 5.

sin and renews a sense of intimacy with Him. I believe this is the tangible "cleansing from unrighteousness" that is described in 1 John 1:9.

When confessing sin to God or others, don't minimize or explain it away. Also, don't try to make it bigger than it is to prove you're sorry. Simply say what you did without explanation and own it before God. Pray something like this, "Father, I confess (say in detail) what I did as a sin against You. I ask You to forgive me of my sin and wash away all spiritual defilement from the sin."

▌ REPENTANCE

Repentance is the turning of your heart towards God and away from darkness (sins or lies). At the heart level, repentance is a choice to love and agree with God with all your being. You can set your heart and shift your affections towards God, His truth, and His righteousness through repentance. Repentance is powerful because it breaks spiritual agreement with darkness and aligns your inner man with God's kingdom. I picture repentance as choosing to get out of a fleshly river with its strong current and getting into the Spirit's river with its strong current. Repentance positions you to walk in the current (the power) of the Spirit a little more each time you make the choice.

Repentance follows confession because you commit to pursuing loving obedience in the area that you confess to God as a sin or lie. Pray something like this, "Father, I turn away from my sin (speak out your sin), and I turn my heart towards You. I set my heart to walk in obedience in this area with Your help. I set my heart to war against this sin with Your help."

> *For thus says the High and Lofty One… I dwell in the high and holy place, with him who has a contrite and humble spirit, to revive the spirit of the humble, and to revive the heart of the contrite ones.*—Isaiah 57:15

Jesus is tender, and a gentleman, and will never force you to "give up" or repent of anything that you want to hold onto. But if you are done holding on to sin or pain or darkness, He is willing and able to free you. Notice here I didn't say that you have to be 100% brave and 100% free from fear going into a prayer time to get freedom; you just have to have a willing heart and say yes to Him in your weakness.

This is a bold statement, but it's been true, I have never seen someone who is hungry and humble not experience deliverance and inner healing. The few who haven't received deliverance in a prayer time weren't interested in repenting of the sins God highlighted; therefore, God couldn't set them free. Choosing to repent of sin is necessary, and when someone isn't willing to repent, the deliverance session should stop because there's no way forward until they are willing.[8]

PERSONAL TESTIMONIES

When I (Bethany) was in Bible school, I heard about deliverance and experienced my first prayer session. I went into my deliverance time prepared with a list of what God highlighted to me. The patterns were that I felt shut down in front of most people and had uneasy emotions when I was with people because I was fearful of their opinions about me. I spoke and thought negatively about my personality and body.

During my deliverance session, the prayer team and I brought these symptoms to God one by one, asking Him to highlight the time each of them began. As we did this, I suddenly remembered a few things that had been said or done to me in my past. At least three memories came up during our prayer time.

The first memory was when I was 18 months old. Because of respiratory sickness, I was placed in a plastic tent for about twenty-four hours without being held or comforted. I didn't remember that experience affecting me emotionally, but it seemed like God wanted to bring comfort to my heart and show me where He was when I didn't know what was going on. When the leaders led me through a prayer of asking God where He was in that hospital room, God showed me a picture of Him coming close to me in the tent. He watched me and held me when no one else was allowed to. What He communicated to me with that picture took that negative memory and filled it with comfort and peace.

The second memory was the day my little brother was born, and I was sad, confused, and scared about seeing my mom on the hospital bed. In the memory, God comforted my adult heart with the truth that He had seen and ministered to me at that young age and that He (and my parents!) were there when I felt scared and alone. I broke agreement with fear and rejection and every scheme of the enemy that began at the time of those

8 Pablo Bottari, *Free in Christ—Your Complete Handbook on the Ministry of Deliverance.* (Lake Mary, FL: Charisma House, 1999), 109.

memories. During that prayer time, the fears of rejection, of my mom dying, and the fear of being replaced by my brother were all healed.

The third memory was when I was five years old, and someone said a few negative words about my body. It was a comment I and others joked about for many years. After I told everyone in the prayer time the memory, I started crying! Then I was embarrassed because it seemed too small to make me cry, so it all caught me off guard. I had to acknowledge that it was a painful comment that did affect me. I broke agreement with the negative comments, forgave the person that said it, and asked God for the truth of what He thought about me and my body. God truly ministered to my heart in the process. Afterwards, my thoughts and emotions felt freer as God told me He saw me, cared about me, and loved me for all that I was. I no longer felt uneasy in my emotions in front of people, and negative thoughts about my personality and body no longer plagued me.

■ WEEKLY ASSIGNMENT

For the next three weeks, you will receive deliverance prayer. You can receive prayer from your Discipleship Mentor or a local ministry that is experienced in deliverance prayer similar to what is described in this chapter. If necessary, one international ministry I recommend utilizing is Bethel Church's Sozo ministry that has a long track record of praying through deliverance and training people. They have a global network of trained leaders that might be in your region. If you haven't already, schedule a 2-hour deliverance prayer session for each of the next three weeks.

LEADERS DELIVERANCE GUIDE

The following steps seek to bring freedom to people in a compassionate way. We desire to reflect the love of Jesus in how we pray, minimizing pain, discomfort, and shame while also addressing the roots of the bondage, which enables the individual to remain free. The prayer time reinforces the authority that the individual has in Christ—we simply agree and partner with them as they arise in the authority Jesus has given.

When you are in the actual prayer time, keep a piece of paper out to take notes. When God highlights a memory to the person, write it down. Next, write down the sins, lies, or injustices that are highlighted within the memory. Give space in between each memory so that you can thoroughly pray through steps three and four until there are measures of breakthrough.

STEP #1 - ASK - DISCUSS THE PERSON'S PRAYER NEEDS.

A. Locate the symptom(s) that the person is dealing with and wants to be free of. Allow the person to set the tone for what God is doing in them. They can get clarity on this prior to the prayer time. Ask, "What are your symptoms? What do you need freedom from?"

B. **Prayer**—Before you begin to pray through the symptom, calmly command every spirit to submit to the Lordship of Jesus. ***"In the name of Jesus, we command every demon to submit to Jesus. We say that you will not manifest in this room or in our hearts in any way."*** Pray for God to increase in the room and have the person receiving prayer pray out their desires for the session.

STEP #2 - REVEAL - ALLOW GOD TO REVEAL AREAS OF OPPRESSION.

A. In prayer together, ask the Spirit to highlight to them: any of the 3 open doors connected to the symptoms.

1. **Sins** they have committed or responses to the abuse, etc.
2. **Injustices** that they need healing from in order to get free.
3. **Lies** they have believed and agreement they have had with the enemy.

Pray until they have thoughts, or a memory connected to their symptoms. Ask them if the Lord said anything or if thoughts are coming to their mind. Take notes and write down what they say and if you sense God highlighting anything. Closer to the end of this step, you can humbly and loosely submit anything you received to them, but let the person confirm or deny what you suggest, and mostly rely on them hearing God.

If a few memories were highlighted, begin with the one that either had the most emotion on it, the one they want to begin with, or simply the earliest memory in their life.

STEP #3 – REPENT – BREAK AGREEMENT WITH DARKNESS.

A. **Confess/Repent of any sins** they committed that were highlighted – Have them pray or lead them in prayer and repent and ask God's forgiveness for sins they have done.

B. **Break agreement with lies** – Allow Him to guide them in turning away from lies. If it's not apparent, ask the Holy Spirit what are the lies they have been believing? And wait until they hear from Him. After lies are located, they can pray to break agreement with the lie themselves, but some might need help doing this.

C. **Forgive from the heart** – Forgive the people involved, themselves, and God. Help them if they are struggling and keep it simple. Don't rush into forgiveness if you sense they are first needing to be comforted by God in the memory. Sometimes it is helpful to ask God where He was before forgiving, so they can feel God's ministry and comfort and safety.

D. **Break agreement with demons** – Have them verbally renounce their agreement with the demonic oppression associated with their symptoms by having them speak something like this: *"In the name of Jesus, I break my agreement with all demons connected to these lies and sins in my life. I close all spiritual doors, and I say no to these lies and sin patterns."*

STEP #4 – PROPHESY TRUTH – ALLOW GOD TO SPEAK HIS TRUTH.

A. **Pray for Healing** – Pray for the person to receive healing from the effects of sins committed against them and forgiveness and healing for the effects of the sins they have committed—inviting God to come into every area.

B. **God's Response** – Ask God to come with forgiveness and comfort, let Him remove and come into emotional pain, bring inner healing, and speak His truth. *Note: Inner healing will occur over time so don't feel pressure to get His full perspective over them. You cannot cast out pain, so help them direct their loss, grief, and pain to Jesus.*

1. Ask God to let the person see how He felt/feels for them. Allow space for Him to speak/prophesy over the person and do what He needs to. Pray for Him to speak, then wait so that person can hear.

2. Usually, if the person cannot hear from God there might be more doors to shut. If there feels like a block or a wall where the person cannot hear God's perspective, stop and ask God together what is hindering the person from receiving truth.

3. If there isn't a tangible emotional feeling of love, peace, or joy from Him, or if they don't feel Him speaking quite yet, go back to Step 2 and Step 3. If nothing is tangible, there could be more open doors that need to be highlighted and opposed. If this session doesn't give time for this, have the individual do this in their personal prayer life and/or schedule another deliverance session.

4. If there is time, pray through other highlighted open doors and do Step 3 and 4 again.

STEP #5 – REBUKE – COMMAND THE DEMONS TO LEAVE.

A. **Rebuke after all doors are closed** – Rebuking and casting out a demon should only be done after they have responded to all the things God highlights. When it seems like God has stopped highlighting things, and the person receiving prayer has been feeling freedom in the prayer time, rebuke the demon. Demons have to leave when all the legal doors have been closed and they are commanded to leave the property. If there are still legal doors to close, the demons have a legal right to stay, so casting them out too early will be less effective.

B. **What it feels like** – When a demon is cast out, there should not be any demonic manifestations (shaking, vomiting, coughing, nausea, choking, fear). If there is, command every spirit to be bound again. When demons leave, there is usually an experience of God's presence, a feeling of heaviness lifting off, and an emotional peace. The person may cry or feel the desire to worship Jesus out of relief and gratitude.

C. **End prayer session** – Once you feel like things are finished within the highlighted open doors, you can have all leaders pray, prophesy over, and bless the person. End the session by thanking God for what was done. Take appropriate notes in order to pick back up where you left off for their potential next deliverance session.

D. **Spiritual Plan** – Help them make a plan to get rid of anything connected to their sins–items used in occult worship, drugs, pornography, and other sin patterns. They should also commit to continuing their prayer schedule, meditating on appropriate Bible passages to counteract the lies they are struggling with, and staying in a community of believers.

22

WALKING OUT FREEDOM: PRAYER

(WRITTEN BY BETHANY MOOTZ)

▌ AFTER PRAYER MINISTRY

After receiving deliverance prayer, there are several things to be aware of to maintain your new freedoms and build up godly strongholds. This includes understanding demonic strategies, continuing the lifestyle of praying through heart issues, and making life changes as a response to the things you've been freed from. Maintaining freedom also consists of building up godly strongholds through prayer and growing in community and accountability in your local church.

RESIST DISCOURAGEMENT

Being confident of this very thing, that He who has begun a good work in you will complete it until the day of Jesus Christ.—Philippians 1:6

After a deliverance session, it will be common for you to be more aware of the heart issues that God's been highlighting. You might feel like the issue is still there, is partly gone, or completely removed. Either way, don't be discouraged! Thank God for what He has done and stay with the process for more freedom. God can break down thick walls in a two-hour prayer time, but pursuing freedom includes setting up multiple prayer sessions, living out a lifestyle of prayer and meditation in an intentional godly community.

For a righteous man may fall seven times and rise again, But the wicked shall fall by calamity.—Proverbs 24:16

Building up a godly stronghold to replace any stronghold of lies takes time. God delights in the process and so can you! Give yourself the grace to be weak; not being passive in addressing your heart issues but understanding you might stumble in the process. There's grace to stumble, and there's grace to get up again and again unto victory. Within the journey, let God lavish His love on you. He wants to be close, and you shouldn't push Him away because you think you aren't clean enough. In the humility of receiving God's joy in the maturing process, you can enjoy His nearness and surrender to His radical love.

INTERNAL STRONGHOLD VS. EXTERNAL ATTACK

There is a difference between an outside demonic attack versus an internal stronghold of lies. In general, external attacks are less powerful, less frequent, and easier to discern as demonic than internal strongholds. God's way to deal with external attacks is to acknowledge, confess, and rebuke the lies you are feeling to God and the people in your life. Repent of anything needed. As you break off the lies, position yourself to receive God's supernatural life into your heart to help you.

If you are having to rebuke the same lie or resist the same level of sin day after day, this could be a clue that you are still dealing with an internal stronghold of lies, which means that somewhere you have agreed with this lie and the demon has authority to lie to you. These consistent lies need to be addressed and prayed through to complete the deliverance.

DELIVERANCE LIFESTYLE

Receiving deliverance prayer from a group is really helpful because of the family dynamic in the Spirit, but we want you to be empowered to pray through things in your alone times as a lifestyle. A simple way to begin this is to have a certain day each week or month where you ask God, "Where and what do I need alignment in?" In these times, God will highlight sins that need to be repented of, new or old lies that you've been believing again, and places where you've been hurt and need to release forgiveness.

Your heart will increase in health if you keep talking to Jesus about your hurts and issues. If praying about this weekly sounds too overwhelming, start with once every one to two months. Set a reminder on your phone, and take one hour to align your heart, repent, confess, forgive, and recommit to what God desires you to be like. These "alignment days" are my favorite because Jesus always ministers to my heart in a refreshing and healing way.

As an example, in one of these alignment times, God highlighted multiple people to forgive. I slowly forgave each person in each circumstance until I felt pain, anger, and unforgiveness lift from my emotions. As my heart experienced freedom, I connected to God's love and compassion for them and started praying blessings over them and our friendships.

In my life, God has tenderly and intimately highlighted things that need to be addressed through confession and repentance. It's a good feeling when He asks me to consider where I am wrong or who I need to forgive in certain situations. I have learned that His correction is His Fatherly love, and that it makes me grow. Moving forward, God wants you to have the perspective that He cares for you and will keep you in alignment with His heart as a tender Father.

BUILDING UP GODLY STRONGHOLDS

You can maintain your freedom and grow in freedom by building godly strongholds. After tearing down demonic strongholds, Jesus wants to build up a strong fortress of truth inside of you. Building these godly strongholds takes time, but you can partner with Jesus to accelerate the process. If you focus on the Word as your spiritual weapon and utilize what you've learned about prayer in the past modules, the fruit of your deliverance prayer sessions will be multiplied.

PRACTICAL CHANGES

> *Therefore do not let sin reign in your mortal body, that you should obey it in its lusts. And do not present your members as unrighteousness to sin.*
> —Romans 6:12-13

If your right eye causes you to sin, pluck it out and cast it from you; for it is more profitable for you that one of your members perish, than for your whole body to be cast into hell. And if your right hand causes you to sin, cut it off and cast it from you; for it is more profitable for you that one of your members perish, than for your whole body to be cast into hell.—Matthew 5:29-30

If you have a weakness in your life, it will benefit you to get rid of the things that trip you up in that area. In conversation with Jesus, consider each broken pattern you prayed through in your deliverance sessions and ask God what stumbling blocks you can get rid of. God admires and encourages you to use godly violence or aggressiveness in removing the hindrances in your life.

Jesus' advice to pluck out eyes and cut off hands applies to perversion and adultery but also to every area of temptation, whether lies or sins. Yes, if you tend to look at things on your phone that you shouldn't, get rid of it at all costs. But if you waste hours viewing "innocent" things, consider ending your subscriptions and setting up godly boundaries in your life. If you tend to say or think ungodly things around certain people, consider changing friends. Some changes can seem severe or too hard, but Jesus' exhortation implies costliness and challenge. However, in the costliness of change, know that the pleasures and freedoms you will experience in the Lord will far surpass what you lay down.

Do not be deceived, God is not mocked; for whatever a man sows, that he will also reap. For he who sows to his flesh will of the flesh reap corruption, but he who sows to the Spirit will of the Spirit reap everlasting life. And let us not grow weary while doing good, for in due season we shall reap if we do not lose heart.—Galatians 6:7-9

In Galatians 6, Paul describes the principle of sowing and reaping that gives insight into your spiritual life. Whatever a man sows in his daily life, he will reap in the next season. This means your current spiritual and emotional life are the fruit of what you sowed during your previous season. The confronting reality of Galatians is that nothing is neutral. We're either sowing seeds towards spiritual fruit or fleshly fruit through each day with our lifestyle choices and thoughts. This is probably why Paul said to take "every" thought captive because every thought is a seed and has future impact if allowed to grow.[1]

Within this sowing and reaping principle, seemingly small or "innocent" non- sinful things can be subtle seeds towards the growth of your flesh. Likewise, small lifestyle choices towards God will multiply a harvest of freedom and godliness. As you make life changes to sow into your spiritual freedom, heed the exhortation of Galatians 6:9, "*let us not grow weary while doing good, for in due season we shall reap if we do not lose heart.*"

Are you reaping negative fleshly things you've sown? Are you depressed? Bored? Dissatisfied? Anxious? Angry? Discontent? Or are you "reaping" God's peace and life on a day-to-day basis by "sowing" prayer, fasting, meditation, and time in the Word, cultivating friendships with other believers, and denying your flesh? It is worth intentionally changing your lifestyle to walk and sow in the Spirit, and it will greatly benefit you because these are the things that build up godly strongholds.

SATISFACTION IN PRAYER

As with any relationship, consistent time with God keeps you grounded and connected to His heart. Disconnection with God is the enemy of continued freedom. If you need power from an electrical outlet, you have to stay engaged or connected to the electric outlet to get the power consistently. Likewise, your daily prayer times with Jesus are how you plug into the power outlet of God. Now, more than ever, it is important to keep your prayer schedule, to engage at a heart level with Jesus (not just a checklist mentality) and hear Him speak His love into you.

A major part of getting and maintaining freedom is experiencing satisfaction and fascination in God's presence. Many sins and broken patterns are healed just by finding satisfaction in God because many areas of brokenness are wrongly trying to satisfy God-given longings. Remember, your most basic need is the spirit of revelation, the experiential knowledge of God's heart. I'm telling you, strongholds crumble when your heart is moving and crying daily in God's presence. I greatly value counseling and programs as a means to freedom and wholeness, but what if you started by giving God more time every day and truly getting a flowing heart? In this discipleship program, you're being equipped to pray one to two hours a day because this amount of time seems like a minimum

---

[1] 2 Corinthians 10:5.

amount of time needed to begin experiencing God in transforming ways. Wherever you're at in your level of desire for God and amount of time with God, I encourage you to re-evaluate how much prayer time you can get each day. If you're closer to one hour a day, consider increasing it by fifteen to thirty minutes every day for now, and then consider moving towards two hours a day in the next few months.

Pursuing this amount of time isn't religious or legalistic; it's a basic relationship principle in the kingdom of God. In my personal life, with kids, work, and life's demands, I know that I need at least two hours a day with God to get my heart flowing and growing. In my marriage, we both understand that we need long amounts of time with God, so every day, we alternate who gets a few hours of prayer and who is responsible for the kids when they wake up. Because of this reality, the weekends aren't sleep-in days; they are opportunities to get more time in prayer to encounter the beautiful God!

BIBLE MEDITATION

Because meditation is the primary way to engage with and encounter God, continuing your specific verse meditations is critical. After deliverance, meditation will position you to be satisfied in God, strengthen you to resist old patterns, and build godly strongholds. Small agreements with God's truth in meditation times will be putting one brick on top of another to build strong walls of truth. If your deliverance times have served to dismantle demonic walls and blinders, now is the time to go deep in the heart of God through meditation without the barriers that once hindered your heart from experiencing truth.

PERSONAL PRAYER LIST

Having a personal prayer list and scheduling weekly times to pray through it is another tool in fighting lies. I suggest putting your main heart issues on your prayer list and seriously praying for them every week. This is so simple but so powerful! Take a few minutes and pray in tongues while asking God for truth or strength in your heart issue. Ask Him to deliver you from temptation and to give you strength. Rebuke demonic attacks from even happening in these areas. Review your prayer list and Bible meditation verse every couple of months and change them depending on what truths you're pursuing.

A few years ago, I (Bethany) felt the Lord highlighting the fear of man as an issue in my life. In response to what He was highlighting, I meditated on key verses to fill me with truth in context to fear of man, and I put "freedom from fear of man" on my daily prayer list.[2] For a few months, I prayed in tongues over my heart crying out for a breakthrough. In those prayer times, I received God's burden for full freedom for myself and felt His zeal and emotions for me.

One day, I was with a person who normally intimidated me and caused me to fear their opinions of me. In discussion, they said something small that I didn't agree with. I normally would have crumpled inside and smiled and nodded on the outside because I was afraid of their rejection and their reaction in every way. However, I felt God saying, "Bethany, stop smiling and disagree with them out loud." I resisted, but God continued, "No, it's ok, disagree with them." I shared my perspective and disagreed with them without being angry or fearful, and this person agreed with me. I almost fell over! I felt like a part of the stronghold of the fear of man was knocked down that day. I pursued more freedom in that season but praying for myself and stepping out that day was a huge starting point, and it made me confident in the fruitfulness of the intentional pursuit of freedom.

▮ WEEKLY ASSIGNMENT

For this week's assignment, take 30-60 minutes in one of your prayer times to ask God who you need to forgive (refer to the personal deliverance section). Close your eyes and ask God to bring people to mind that you need to forgive. When a person comes to mind, you will probably know what you need to forgive them for. Out loud to God, forgive them for the specific things they did or said until peace replaces the emotions of pain and anger. If you don't feel anything change in your emotions, continue to talk to God about the situation, speak forgiveness again, and pray blessings over them. If God brings more people to mind than you have time for, schedule another forgiveness prayer time.

---

[2] Zephaniah 3:16-17; Galatians 1:10.

23

WALKING OUT FREEDOM: CHURCH FAMILY

(WRITTEN BY BETHANY MOOTZ)

COMMUNITY AND ACCOUNTABILITY

From whom the whole body, joined and knit together by what every joint supplies, according to the effective working by which every part does its share, causes growth of the body for the edifying of itself in love.—Ephesians 4:16

In this hour of history, God is restoring the definition and glory of the local church as His primary means of transforming believers and society. God has strategically placed a significant piece of your freedom in the people that make up your local church. Churches are meant to be places of deep friendships that pursue God together and edify (build up) each other in love. If you haven't already, now is the time to focus on building deep spiritual friendships within your church and posturing your heart to receive all the discipleship you can receive from your leaders.

"WITH THOSE"

Flee also youthful lusts; but pursue righteousness, faith, love, peace with those who call on the Lord out of a pure heart.—2 Timothy 2:22

God has ordained Biblical community and relational accountability to be a weapon against the darkness, and a tool for believers to walk in personal freedom. In my opinion, you will grow twice as fast if you deeply engage in a hungry community of believers. To a degree, we pursue righteousness alone, but in 2 Timothy 2:22, there's another place for pursuing righteousness in your church community "with those who call on the Lord out of a pure heart." We are exhorted to flee sinful desires and pursue righteousness with like-minded people who have hungry and pure hearts because they will provoke us, convict us, talk us into more righteousness, and encourage us along the way.

CONFESSING TO OTHERS

Some people think that if they're open to God, they don't have to be open or confess to other people, but that isn't how God set it up. When you are open with others, your heart is more open with God. The capacity of your heart to love Jesus and to fulfill your destiny increases according to your openness to your church community. I tell young people that are not in a true community that they're only going to reach fifty percent of their spiritual destiny alone. Our spiritual growth and deliverance are deeply connected to our level of friendship with other wholehearted believers.

And if he has committed sins, he will be forgiven. Confess your trespasses to one another, and pray for one another, that you may be healed.—James 5:15-16

God already knows you have sinned and will forgive you if you ask Him to, but the Biblical value is that it has to be exposed on the human level before you can receive full healing and breakthrough from God. It is through vulnerability with others that healing flows. Jesus paid for the cleansing of your sins already but will apply more cleansing as you confess and repent to others in your community.

When things remain in darkness, our perspectives and wrong thinking are allowed to stay. But when we confess and expose hidden things, we allow truth to flood our souls. I'm not talking about shouting your sins from the rooftops. I'm talking about being transparent with a trust-filled, safe environment where you know and do life with the people you are confessing to; those who will hold you accountable to getting out of sin and love you in the midst of your weakness.

You are vulnerable to demonic swirls of accusation when you are isolated because God never meant for us to be alone. These same accusations can only be broken off through God's gift to us, which is community. Godly relationships are where people are calling each other to greater places of loving God and each other and breaking through life circumstances together.

We desperately need God to point out our blind spots and bring inner healing where we've been hurt by people. There are many hindrances to having community and friendships: past hurt relationships and not wanting to be hurt again, wrong perspectives (I have to wait and be pursued instead of initiating a relationship), fear of being known in weakness or sin, I don't have time for it, I don't know how to be a friend or be friendly to people, etc. Ask God for the humility to see where you need an alignment or a deeper healing work so that you can begin to see from His perspective the gift of grafting into your church community.

God wants us to form friendships around prayer, fasting, the Word, and the spirit of revelation. If friendships are not formed around pursuing God together, they will not be life-giving or Biblical. If you go deep in God with other people, your discussions will center around who God is and what He is doing in each of you. I believe these kinds of friendships are within the definition of what church is supposed to be—a group of committed friends intentionally pursuing God together in deep relationship.

In a church community, you will have conflict. The lack of perfection in any community is guaranteed. No community does relationships perfectly. You will want to keep the deep places of your heart hidden for fear of rejection and shame. You will not want to forgive and respond in humility towards a sincere but weak brother who hurt you. But if you desire wholeheartedness and to continue receiving breakthroughs from the Lord, you need one another and you need committed loving relationships.

All of us have an excuse as to why we hide little things, but if you are not going to be open, you are closing your heart off from receiving from the very community you are a part of. You're also hindering the community from true unity. If you do not open up, who will? The hard parts of community life shouldn't hinder us from wanting and desiring to be a part of the culture of a community where vulnerability and accountability are celebrated, and weakness is handled Biblically.

PRAYER ACCOUNTABILITY

Prayer accountability is having a regular checkpoint with a few people of mutual commitment to confess sins, encourage each other in spiritual pursuits, and pray for each other. Prayer accountability can best happen with companions in the faith, people you see regularly and can run alongside you and pick you up when you fall, and vice versa. Right now, you have this with your Discipleship Mentor, but God wants this for you for every season, however it looks. If you've never had this type of relationship before, pray about what people might be a good fit for you when you transition out of this program. The best place to look for someone who could be a prayer accountability partner is in your current local church.

A simple model for prayer accountability is to discuss each person's spiritual pursuits: prayer life (prayer/fasting schedule, meditation verse, Bible study direction), heart issues, and gifting. The *Spiritual Pursuits Document* in this program is set up to be used for future accountability friendships. Set up a regular meeting time, and then decide what they want to share and be accountable for. Ask each person to share what God has been doing in their heart through prayer and the Word, how they've been doing with walking out their prayer schedule, how they've been doing with their heart issue, and how they are growing in their giftings. Encourage the group to listen, ask good questions, encourage, challenge, prophesy, and release God's forgiveness when sins and weaknesses are confessed.

Through relational accountability, you can more easily overcome sin patterns and heart issues, feel the heart of God as you are loved and accepted in your weaknesses, extend the merciful forgiving heart of God to others, and learn to be vulnerable and open with no shame or hiding. There is profound grace to grow with accountability as you confess openly to those who know all your weaknesses, and time after time, they still love you and cheer you on. Confession can be more than sharing sins. It can include confessing doubts, fears, struggles, pain, but also truths and victories!

█ WEEKLY ASSIGNMENT

Besides continuing to pray through your heart issues this week, take some time to consider your understanding of God's plans for the local church. Answer the following questions. *How involved and connected are you with your church family? Based on Ephesians 4:12 and 16, What does it mean to be edified and to edify others in your church? What does is look like to have deep spiritual friendships in your church? What could a prayer accountability friendship look like for you?*

MODULE 6

BIBLE STUDY

MODULE INTRODUCTION

Before getting into this module, I want to encourage you that your passion for God and your yes to daily prayer moves God's heart, even if your yes feels small most days. God is looking for friends on the earth who give Him the time and love He deserves, and He's finding that in you. In addition, the way you're pursuing prayer is the wisest thing you can do in this hour of history. What you are cultivating in God will be your strength and life source in every season and will be the very thing you lead others into.

The purpose of this Bible study module is to give you the vision, confidence, and tools you need to go deep in the study of the Word of God. You will learn the practicals of how to pursue the Biblical truths God highlights to you in each season, which is one of this program's primary goals. You will also learn about three different study approaches (general reading, topical studies, and book studies), how to do word studies, and how to utilize study resources (Bible study websites, commentaries, Bible dictionaries, Greek/Hebrew resources).

The module assignments include a topical study, a study on a book of the Bible, and a word study. These assignments will train you to do in-depth study on topics that are relevant to you moving forward, but personalize the assignments by using them to study the truths you are pursuing right now. In preparation, review your *Spiritual Pursuits Document* and determine if anything needs to be changed, and pick your study and meditation direction. I suggest studying and meditating within the same truth, and possibly even within the same verses so that you can focus and go deep through both means.

ASSIGNMENT OVERVIEW
MODULE 6 – BIBLE STUDY

Continue to follow your prayer schedule and Spiritual Pursuits each week. As a follow-up to the deliverance module, continue to pray through heart issues during part of each Discipleship Mentor meeting. Also, schedule an Extended Group Prayer Day (2-4 hours) for week 28 or 29.

Week Twenty-six Assignments:

❑ Read Chapter 24 – "***Bible Study Approaches.***" Journal your thoughts and questions about the chapter.

❑ Begin the Topical Study assignment. This is a two-week assignment.

❑ Fill out a new *Spiritual Pursuits Document* for this module. The pursuits can stay the same or change but filling out the form monthly helps you refocus and develop a rhythm of intentionality.

Week Twenty-seven Assignments:

❑ No chapter reading this week.

❑ Complete your Topical Study assignment.

❑ Schedule an Extended Group Prayer Day for week 28 or 29.

❑ **Meet with your Discipleship Mentor.**

Week Twenty-eight Assignments:

❑ Read Chapter 25 – "***Book Study Part 1.***" Journal your thoughts and questions about the chapter.

❑ Begin your Book Study assignment (research the book's background, read the book through several times, and create a general outline). This is a three-week assignment.

Week Twenty-nine Assignments:

❑ Read Chapter 26 – "***Book Study Part 2.***" Journal your thoughts and questions about the chapter.

❑ Continue your Book Study assignment by going more in-depth (2-3 more layers) on your existing outline. Finish this detailed outline this week.

❑ **Meet with your Discipleship Mentor.**

Week Thirty Assignments:

- ❑ No chapter reading this week.
- ❑ Finish your Book Study assignment by writing your own commentary on each verse within one section of verses (5-10 verses).

Week Thirty-one Assignments:

- ❑ Read Chapter 27 – "*Word Studies and Interpretation.*" Journal your thoughts and questions about the chapter.
- ❑ Complete your Word Study assignment.
- ❑ Write down a 1–2-month Bible study plan to put in the next module's *Spiritual Pursuits Document.*
- ❑ **Meet with your Discipleship Mentor.**

SPIRITUAL PURSUITS   *DATE:* _____

1. **Bible reading direction and plan**
   (Write down what you will read and when you will read it):

2. **Meditation verse** (Choose a verse that speaks truth into your heart issue):

3. **Sin/character issue from which to get freedom:**

4. **Lie from which to pursue deliverance:**

5. **Gifting to pursue** (Include simple ways you can pursue it):

6. **Weekly Prayer Schedule**—Write down your plan for the *specific times* you are committed to spending with God each day, and *what specifically you plan to do during those times*. Include what your study or meditation focus will be. Refer to the example schedule in Chapter Two. (e.g., Monday 6-6:30 am—Tongues, 6:30-7:30 am—Meditation on Song of Solomon 1:2)

Monday

Tuesday

Wednesday

Thursday

Friday

Saturday

Sunday

24

BIBLE STUDY APPROACHES

MEDITATION AND STUDY

God wants to bring Bible study and meditation together in your life. It is normal for them to be pitted against each other, or for personality types to gravitate towards one or the other, but they are meant to flow together and fuel one another. Bible study will help you understand the fuller context and meaning of a Bible topic, while meditation will position you to encounter God in the truth in a deeper way. Bible study gives you information and understanding to meditate on, and meditation brings up questions to study. Both aspects are forms of searching out God's heart, and both are needed to experience transformation.

If you maintain the meditative heart posture you've been cultivating in this program, you will be able to healthily grow in intimacy with God in Bible study. You will be challenged by the focus and thought the study assignments will require, but you'll be blessed by your labors. I encourage you to enter into the initial tension of Bible study and meditation and to find your way in it without abandoning one or the other.

WHY STUDY THE BIBLE

GOD'S HEART REVEALED

The Bible is the revelation of the heart of God written down for us to engage with, and when we talk to God about it, light fills our understanding and transforms us. As a Person with real thoughts, emotions, and desires, God has revealed Himself in the Bible and wants to be known by us. He wants to take the written Word and make it the Living Word by releasing encounters with Jesus. When we talk about Bible study, it means to study and peer into God's personality, values, and His ways so that we can know Him and become more like Him as His bride.

Sometimes Christians automatically slip into a non-relational academic mindset when they think about the idea of Bible study. Deep down, they believe it's merely a mental pursuit of right Christian doctrines and principles. You can be a believer and still approach Bible study in a non-relational way, but this doesn't have to be the case for you. If you can keep the perspective that you're pursuing God's heart from the place of longing, and that you can keep a meditative posture while studying, you can see Bible study as being relational and similar to meditation. This perspective will allow your desire for God to express itself in the form of searching Him out in Bible study.

> *"You search the Scriptures, for in them you think you have eternal life; and these are they which testify of Me. But you are not willing to come to Me that you may have life."*—John 5:39-40

Jesus rebuked the religious leaders of His day for studying the Scriptures without a relational perspective. They searched out His plans through study, but they weren't willing to talk to God about the things they were studying, and they were not willing to obey the Spirit's leading. Jesus rebuked their approach. He desired that they would find life in Him through prayerful study. This passage does not discourage Bible study; it encourages conversation and encounter with God in Bible study, and it promises intimacy and life.

JESUS AND THE APOSTLES

Going deep in the Bible includes meditation and study because the two flow together in searching out God. The apostles valued both and gave most of their ministry time to

Bible study, meditation, and prayer so they could experience God and know His values.[1] We know they had Biblical depth because they were people who understood God's kingdom and the Messiah before Jesus called them to be disciples. They continued their pursuit of the scriptures after Jesus' ascension so they could form the early church around new revelations. The New Testament writings are a fruit of their Biblical understanding.

As the Son of God, Jesus valued the role of study and meditation in under- standing His Father and knowing His ways. As a Jewish boy in Galilee, He would have grown up memorizing the Torah and learning through meditation and study.[2] By the age of twelve, He had cultivated enough understanding of the scriptures to dialogue with Jewish teachers in the temple and amaze those around Him.[3] Jesus equated Bible study with knowing what His Father was doing, *"Did you not know that I must be about My Father's business?"*[4]

Jesus displayed the fruit of His Biblical understanding throughout His entire life. In the wilderness, He used His Biblical depth to discern and war against Satan's lies and temptations.[5] In His teaching ministry, Jesus brought new understanding and new interpretations to the Bible and amazed people with His wisdom and authority. Through study and communion with His Father, He understood His role as Messiah from Biblical prophecies, and He knew His Father's timing for the cross, the resurrection, and His second coming.

BUILT-UP BY THE WORD

"So now, brethren, I commend you to God and to the word of His grace, which is able to build you up and give you an inheritance among all those who are sanctified."—Acts 20:32

There are three phrases in Acts 20:32 that are significant regarding the power of the Word. In context, Paul spoke this to the Ephesian elders for the last time. In this meeting, he entrusted them to the power of God in His Word as their means of growth.

---

[1] 1 Acts 6:2, 4.

[2] Luke 2:40.

[3] Luke 2:46-47.

[4] Luke 2:49.

[5] Matthew 4:3-10.

Paul called the Bible "the word of His grace." God's Word releases grace and transforming power to the human heart. Engaging Him in the Word is the source of receiving His empowering grace in your thoughts, emotions, and desires.

His Word is "able to build you up." His Word has the supernatural ability to build up your heart in the Spirit. In module four, you learned that praying in tongues builds you up, but His Word also builds up and is the primary way He encounters and edifies the believer. His Word will fill your heart with His fiery love and fascination and awaken your spiritual desires for Him. His Word will wash away lies and accusations and the lusts of the flesh and bring you into a place of truth, righteousness, and empowerment. A built-up soul finds satisfaction in God and grows in distaste for the deceitful pleasures of darkness.

His Word will "give you an inheritance among all those who are sanctified." Your inheritance in God refers to all that He has promised you in this age and in eternity. Paul says that the Bible will give you an inheritance because everything in your life hinges upon you experiencing God's life in the Word. As you fill your heart with His Word, it will renew your thoughts, invigorate your emotions, and set you on a holy course to fulfill your destiny. You will only realize your inheritance if you come to God as the life source, and the starting point is His Word.

Therefore lay aside all filthiness and overflow of wickedness, and receive with meekness the implanted word, which is able to save your souls.—James 1:21

James called the Bible the "implanted word." The Word is like a divine seed that is thrust into the soil of the human heart. In the right conditions, the small seed will take root and produce divine fruitfulness. The implanted word "is able to save your souls." If you give yourself to the Word and respond to the Word in meekness, it will progressively transform and deliver you from brokenness and darkness and renew it into the glorious image of God

You must lay hold of the Word of God with intentionality to experience the glorious promises of fruitfulness. If you're casual in making time for God in the Word, you will end up being in the Word less often, and it will bear less fruit in your soul. But if you carve out time and have a plan, you will give God time and space to awaken your heart. An awakened heart will begin to demand more and more time to feast on the Word of God and lead to transformation and more satisfaction in God.

BIBLE STUDY APPROACHES

There are three approaches to Bible study that I use and suggest to people wanting to grow in the Word. Each one of them has its specific benefits. As you read each description, consider how you could apply them in your study life.

GENERAL READING PLAN

The simplest way to study the Bible is to pick a book or books of the Bible to read on specific days of the week. This is most people's default study approach. The benefit of doing this is that it is so simple and so easy to do that you can quickly get a rhythm in it and enjoy it. Two other benefits of general reading are that you can see the big picture and central themes of a book or Bible section and follow the author's storyline because you're reading it straight through. This simple study method helps grow a hunger for the Word, leading to a desire for more in- depth study. When I have a general reading plan, I connect to the storyline, which helps me pick up my Bible to continue reading when I have a few minutes here and there.

1. Start by deciding what you want to read based on the truths that you want to grow in. Pick one book of the Bible like Romans or Ephesians or pick a section of the Bible like the Gospels, the Psalms, or the entire New Testament. If you're not sure what to read or are not very familiar with the Bible, I would recommend reading through the New Testament several times. You could read it through every two months if you read about five chapters a day.

2. Plan to read a certain number of chapters each day or plan to read for a certain amount of time each day. An example would be to read five chapters a day or to read for an hour a day. If you decide to read one book, depending on its size, you may even be able to read the entire thing each day.

3. Take time to turn what you're reading into conversation with the Lord. When a verse moves you, or you want to say something to the Lord about what you're reading, stop and talk to Him for a minute and then continue reading. These reading times aren't meant to be deep meditation times, but your heart will engage God more and receive more if you have a conversation with Him.

4. Have a notepad with you while you read and write down a few thoughts, questions, observations, and things you would want to study later.

TOPICAL STUDY

Topical Bible study is an approach that focuses on studying the Bible by specific topics. A topical study requires a little more work than just having a general reading plan, but it's still simple and easy for everyone to do. The benefits of this approach are that you can focus on the specific topic you want to study, and you can gather a broad number of verses and information on the subject. This approach is a perfect way to pursue one of the truths you know you need in this season.

A topical study will cultivate a longing for truth and create spiritual momentum in your heart for specific topics. When you search out topics, you naturally engage the parts of your heart that were made to search and discover God. Each day you go deeper into a topic, new layers of truth and understanding will open up. As this happens, you will encounter God in the truth and become hungrier for a fuller understanding. Like searching out a treasure, your heart will want to keep engaging as you see the truth unfolding in front of you.

1. Start by picking one Bible topic that you want to study to help free you from your current heart issue or empower you in a gift you want to grow in.

2. In a topical study, the first step is to gather information on the topic. Start by finding Bible verses on the topic and compiling them in a notepad or on your computer. You can find verses or chapters on your topic in three ways: write down verses you already know of, look up keywords on a Bible website, and look up the topic in a Bible dictionary or Topical Bible. These three extra resources reference verses by topic and give commentary on the topic. The main website I use for word searches, Bible dictionaries, and Topical Bibles is www.studylight.org. I'll guide you in using this specific website, but you can access the same resources on other Bible study websites.

3. Go to www.studylight.org and click "Bible Study Tools" and then select "Bible Concordance (Topical Bibles)," "Bible Dictionary," or "Bible Encyclopedia." I suggest using the International Standard Bible Encyclopedia because it is clear and has extensive information. Enter your topic in the search bar of whatever resource you choose, and then write down the verses they reference in your notepad or computer.

4. After gathering information on the topic, review and study all your verses while writing down your thoughts and specific questions on any verses. Continue to read the verses to find answers to your questions. If there isn't much information or many

verses, this may be a quick study. If there are a lot of verses and outside information, you could take your time over the course of weeks to study and pray through the topic.

EXAMPLE TOPICAL STUDY

If I were to pick forgiveness as my topic, I would type in variations of the word (forgiveness, forgiven, forgive) in the Bible search option on a Bible study website. Then I would copy all the relevant verses into my computer. Afterward, I would go into a Bible Dictionary and Nave's Topical Bible on the website and click on forgiveness as a topic. I would copy all their verses and ideas and copy them in my document. Lastly, I would take several days to look at all of the verses and write down truths and questions from the verses. If there was a key verse, I would consider meditating on it for a while.

Based on my questions, I might need to look up other topics to understand forgiveness better. With the topic of forgiveness, I would want to know how the blood of Jesus allows me to be forgiven. There would be some edifying bunny trails to study within this topic, leading to even more clarity.

BOOK STUDY

A book study is an in-depth study of one book of the Bible. This approach takes the most work, but it's a natural way of learning. It produces a lot of fruit because it's so comprehensive. The benefits are an immersion into the heart and thought process of the book's author and the Holy Spirit, understanding each verse in relation to the entire book, and more easily reading from the original audience's perspective. It is easy to get spiritual momentum in this type of study because you become so immersed in the book's storyline and get excited about seeing all the verses come together.

With the book study approach, you can go as in-depth as you want. The four basic things you need to do are **study the book's background** (author and audience), **discover the overview of the book** (main themes and main points), **create a personal outline** of the book, and **write your own commentary** on each verse or section. You can go as deep as you want in each of these three categories, and you can decide if you want to study the entire book or a specific section of the book.

The process of creating an outline and writing a personal commentary will help you engage the truths of the book. The process will force you to summarize and personalize what you're reading, which produces clarity and a personal response to God. After studying a book, you will be able to tell someone else what the main point of the book is in one sentence, and what each section of the book is saying in one sentence. The process will also help you grow in understanding how each verse connects to the book's main themes, which will help you interpret them better.

IMPLEMENTING BIBLE STUDY

Within your weekly prayer schedule, you have planned times to meditate, worship, pray in tongues, and study the Bible. During this module, review your prayer schedule and see where you want your Bible study times to be and what topic or section of the Bible you want to focus on in those times. If you haven't had a strong Bible reading or Bible study plan so far, this is the module to learn how to do so and put it into place in your times with the Lord.

WHAT

Decide what you want to read or study. I suggest picking part or all your Bible reading based on the truths you need in this season. Bible study and meditation can flow together, so consider doing them both on the same topic or verses. Typically, I have two different Bible study directions in my weekly prayer schedule: one for general reading in a section of the Bible that I'm interested in and another that is specific to what I want my heart to grow in.

WHEN

Decide when you want to study the Bible in your weekly prayer schedule. Do you want or need to find more time to be in the Word each week? In your schedule, write down what days and times you're going to study and what you'll be studying.

HOW

Decide how you want to approach your study. Out of the three approaches in this chapter, which one or two would you want to use for a month or more? Based on the study approaches you pick, write down a few bullet points of how you will study. For example, if you're going to do a topical study on God's love, write down each simple step of what you're going to do. Review your steps whenever you're not sure what to do in your study times.

WEEKLY ASSIGNMENT

The assignment for the next two weeks is to do a topical study and to write down a detailed Bible study plan on how to execute it. In the study plan, write down what you're going to study, what approach you're going to try, and what simple steps you're going to take in the study. Follow the steps in the chapter for your assignment. Two weeks should give you adequate time to find a rhythm in topical studies and get some depth in the topic of your choice.

This assignment is designed to be done during the Bible study days in your prayer schedule. Consider using all your Bible times for two weeks on this assignment so you can go deep. Also, the assignment is meant to be in line with the Bible topics you are already investing in, so choose a topic that you're wanting more truth in right now. Doing so will help you build godly strongholds in place of the demonic strongholds that were torn down in the last module. As you make this personal, it will impact your heart and become a testimony that strengthens you to study after this module.

DISCIPLESHIP MEETING GUIDE
MODULE 6: BIBLE STUDY - CHAPTER 24

MEETING FOCUS:

The purpose of this meeting is to discuss your Topical Study assignment and continue praying through your heart issue.

DISCUSSION QUESTIONS (IN ORDER OF IMPORTANCE):

1. *Heart Issue:*
   a. Share how your heart issue has been going since the deliverance module. Take time together to ask God for more clarity concerning the current heart issue or ask Him to highlight more things to pray through during this meeting. Use the simple deliverance prayer steps from the last module.

2. *Chapter Questions:*
   a. Chapter 24 – Discuss your journaled thoughts and questions from the chapter. Do you struggle with viewing Bible study as only academic and not relational? Do you see how meditation and study can work together?
   b. Topical Study assignment – In-depth, discuss how your assignment went for you and how God impacted your heart. In relation to the deliverance module, do you feel like this study helped build you up in truth?

3. *Spiritual Pursuits:*
   a. Practically, how is your prayer schedule going? How many days have you walked out your prayer schedule? Do you need to make small changes to your schedule? How are your daily prayer times going, and how is God impacting you through them?
   b. Briefly review your new *Spiritual Pursuits Document.*

4. Briefly review the assignments for the next two weeks together.

MEETING NOTES:

_____

_____

_____

_____

_____

_____

_____

_____

_____

_____

_____

_____

25

BOOK STUDY PART ONE

▎EVERYONE CAN GO DEEP

As you begin the book study chapters of this module, I want to encourage you that you are called and able to go deep in Bible study. God has depths available to you in the Word. He's given you the necessary skills to study, and there are abundant Bible resources to help you grow. In my observation, the three things that hold people back from going deep are having enough time, not knowing where to start or how to study, and feeling intimidated and unqualified. All three of these will be easy to overcome if you press in during this module.

FINDING ENOUGH TIME

The first issue is regarding having enough time for Bible study. If you don't have much time scheduled for prayer each day, you are going to feel limited in where you can go in Bible study. If you know this is the case for you, take a fresh look at your weekly schedule and see if you can find more time. That might mean saying no to entertainment or legitimate activities and being more focused in your daily schedule but finding the extra time with God is so worth it!

Consider orienting your life and schedule around getting enough time with God, and then schedule everything else after you've established those sacred times. Resist the temptation of resigning to the amount of time you have with God and take a fresh look at your schedule. Even if you can only find fifteen or thirty more minutes a day to be with Him, it will help you substantially.

Many of you reading this have pursued studies, whether in college or in job training. What if you were to apply the same intensity of study as you did for those pursuits? Jobs and schooling are worthy causes, but how much more worthy is the pursuit of the truth in God's Word?

We all experience hard seasons and have circumstances that seem to hinder us from spending more time with God, but more time with Him is the answer in the midst of hard seasons. God challenged me to spend more time with Him in a tough season when my kids were young, were going through health issues, weren't sleeping well, and our parents were going through severe health challenges. All these situations left me more tired and with less time, which resulted in me pulling back from prayer, fasting, and Bible study. Essentially, I had resigned to less quality time with God.

One day, God interrupted my thoughts and whispered to me, "You have a demon in your life." I said, "What are you talking about? What demon is in my life?" God replied and said, "You have a demon called excuses. All your challenges are real and difficult, and I know what you're going through, but this demon is exploiting them to discourage you from spending more time with Me. He's making your circumstances seem bigger than they really are, and he's convincing you that they are valid excuses for not spending enough time with Me.

I felt the Father's heart in this conversation, and it helped me say no to my legitimate excuses. He communicated that He was fully with me in my challenges, and He didn't dismiss or minimize them. But at the same time, as my Father, He was calling me higher and saying that He would help me. He wasn't just rebuking me out of anger and then leaving me to figure things out by myself.

God said something like, "I know your challenges! They are real! But I will help you spend time with Me. You can fast and pray and be in the Word more in the midst of being tired in your circumstances. I'm with you in this, and I will give you grace!" It's like He came as a father to pick me up from the ground and committed to holding me up as I walked.

KNOWING WHERE TO START

The second issue is learning how to study the Bible and knowing where to start in the process. You can learn how to study, and it doesn't have to be complicated! The most important thing is to decide what you will study for a month or two, and then write down a simple study plan. If you think it through on the front end, you will feel confident during your studies.

Part of the learning process is practicing the study methods in this module, both now and moving forward. You will gain a level of clarity and confidence from doing the assignments, but each time that you use a study approach (general reading, topical study, book study, word study) you will feel clearer and more confident. The more times you practice the different study techniques, the more natural they will be, and the more enjoyable they will be. If you give yourself to utilizing the study approaches this month while you have focus, structure, and mentors, your study growth will accelerate.

The third issue is feeling intimidated and under-equipped to do in-depth Bible study. The idea of understanding the historical settings of the Bible, interpreting verses, and getting into Bible commentaries and other resources can seem intimidating. I relate to feeling intimidated because that's how I felt in my twenties. I never enjoyed studying anything growing up, but when I got saved, there was a desire to dig into the truth. After learning how to study from mentors, the intimidation was removed, and I felt empowered to discover the Bible. You don't have to be super smart or have a theology degree to have Biblical clarity. All you need is the Holy Spirit, a tender heart, time, and a little experience with Bible resources to have a good foundation for understanding and interpreting the Bible.

Some of the intimidation comes from not knowing the Bible or the history of Biblical times. Each year that you study, you will grow in understanding the history of Israel, Jesus' life, and the New Testament contexts. This will only come as you study over time, but it's doable and enjoyable.

OVERVIEW OF BOOK STUDY APPROACH

A book study approach studies one book of the Bible at a time to get immersed in the Holy Spirit's flow of thought. Like a story, each book of the Bible is meant to be read as one piece of truth. The Holy Spirit and human authors wrote their books knowing that each sentence was connected and built upon the ones that came before. Therefore, a book study will bring you into a greater understanding of individual sentences because you will read them in context to the book's central message. You'll also read them in context to the original audience, which is the starting place for interpreting passages and understanding the Spirit's overall message in a book.

The four essential components of a book study are to **study the book's background** (author and audience), **discover the book's overview** (main themes and main points)**, create a personal outline** of the book, and **write your own commentary** on each verse or section.

Creating an outline and writing a personal commentary will help you engage the truths of the book. The process will force you to summarize and personalize what you're reading, which produces clarity and personal responses to God. After studying a book, you will be able to tell others the main point of the book in one sentence, and what each section of the book is saying in one sentence. In all of this, you will get hooked by the life of God you experience through the searching process and the growing connection to the book's storyline, and your appetite for the sweetness of the Word will expand.

STUDY THE BOOK'S BACKGROUND

A book study begins with understanding its background, which includes knowing details about the author. Who were they? When and why did they write the book? What was their relationship like with their readers? It can even be helpful to look at the author's life as a whole to understand their heart and journey. Understanding the background also includes knowing who the original audience was and what they were dealing with at the time of the book's writing.

Most of this background information can be found in Bible resources like Bible dictionaries, Bible Encyclopedias, and in the introduction section of commentaries. If you have a study Bible, it most likely has some background information before each new book of the Bible. Check multiple Bible sources to get as much understanding as possible, and then write down your information in one spot. You don't have to remember or understand all the information, but you will learn more progressively as you do this.

The next step is to understand the overview or big picture of the entire book. As you read, answer the questions: what are the main points and the main themes, what are the repetitive ideas, and how do all the chapters connect to each other? You can get some overview thoughts from the Bible resources, but the primary way is to read, if possible, the entire book in one sitting several times over the course of a week or two. Every time you read the book, you will see the big picture become more apparent, and you will see main themes emerge. As you read, write down all your observations. Observing and writing these things down will help you create an outline.

GENERAL BOOK OUTLINE

A book outline is a document you make that breaks the book up into different- sized sections. The general book outline is the first of three to four layers in the outlining process. In the next chapter, you will learn about the deeper layers of outlining. There are no wrong outlines, and your outline might change later. Typically, I have two different Bible study directions in my weekly prayer schedule: one for general reading in a section of the Bible that I'm interested in and another that is specific to what I want my heart to grow in. The focus is more on the benefits of the outlining process.

Creating an outline is incredibly beneficial because it guides you in a systematic way of praying and thinking through the content and flow of the book. It forces you to ask and answer the question, "What is the author saying, and how is he saying it?" Summarizing each section with a short sentence will help you personalize and own the topic of each section. By the end of the process, you will understand and be able to communicate the book's main points, summarize each section with a sentence, and walk someone through the book's flow.

1. **First outline layer** – For the first outline layer, divide the book into large sections. As a general idea, there may be two to four large sections in a book. You can identify these larger sections by big topic changes.

   In the book of Ephesians, an idea for large sections would be chapters 1-3 as the first section and 4-6 as the second section. The first section is filled with truths of who we are in Christ, and then Paul shifts to more exhortation and application in the second section. In Acts, chapters 1-12 are focused on Peter and the gospel among the Jews, and chapters 13-28 are focused on Paul and the gospel among the Gentiles.

2. **Second outline layer** – To make the second outline layer, divide the large sections into smaller ones. In shorter books, these sections might be the size of one or two chapters. In longer books, these sections might include several chapters. These

smaller sections fit within the broader topic of the large sections, but they have their own focus within that. In a shorter book like Ephesians, chapters 1-3 could be broken up into three sections the size of the chapters or into two sections that are a little larger. In a longer book like Acts, chapters 1-12 could be broken into smaller sections like chapters 1-5 (Jerusalem Church established) and 6-12 (Gospel spreads).

3. **Title each section** – Write a few words or a short sentence to title each section you make. The purpose of the title is to summarize the main point of the section in your own words.

EXAMPLE BOOK STUDY – ACTS

BOOK BACKGROUND

Based on my reading from one commentary and a couple of other Bible resources, I would write down a few paragraphs of information that helped me understand the book. For a serious book study, I would have one to two pages of introductory information written down. The example below would be longer if I copied more paragraphs from a commentary, wrote more about Luke's life, and expanded on the purpose of Luke-Acts.

Luke, a minister with Paul, wrote Acts to go along with the Gospel of Luke. Luke probably wrote the book around 62 AD, when Paul was in prison for two years. The book covers about thirty years of early Church history, from Jesus' resurrection to the end of Paul's ministry. Luke relied on eyewitnesses, written documents, trustworthy oral traditions, and his own understanding of what people preached in the book. The Greek word for "acts" was used to describe famous people's heroic deeds in Greek culture. This book portrays the acts of the Spirit through the apostles.

The Gospel of Luke and Acts were explicitly addressed to Theophilus to prove the existence of Jesus and to teach about Him and His salvation story through the early Church. People believe Theophilus was either a Roman officer learning about Judaism and Jesus or a Jewish leader learning about Jesus with Luke.

Luke wrote these books to prove to Theophilus and other Gentiles the validity of Jesus' life and message through an accurate and detailed account. His writings helped the world understand the gospel of the Jews and why it was being widely accepted among the Gentiles.

BOOK OVERVIEW

I start connecting to the overview or big picture of a book by reading it through in one sitting several times. Acts is a long book, so it takes me about an hour to read at a medium pace. I read slow enough to understand what I'm reading, but not slow enough to catch every detail. As I read, I write down themes, key verses, and ideas of how I would outline. This process is similar to brainstorming in that I put a lot of observations and thoughts on paper, and then I organize them later.

The book's main point seems to be the fulfillment of Jesus' promise to send the Holy Spirit and His impact on the Jews and Gentiles. Luke follows the story of the Spirit as He is poured out and then breaks out in power to bring multitudes into the kingdom. The apostles were filled with the Spirit, and then they brought the Holy Spirit to Jerusalem, Samaria, and the regions beyond. Acts 1:8 summarizes the main point of the book, "But you shall receive power when the Holy Spirit has come upon; and you shall be witnesses to Me in Jerusalem, and in all Judea and Samaria, and to the ends of the earth."

A secondary point of the book seems to be the outworking of Israel's destiny to be a light to the gentile nations. Throughout the book, the Jewish apostles are unsure how their new Messianic faith impacts their laws, religious customs, and the gentile nations around them. In the book, there is a progressive outworking of the Messianic faith. The first half of the book is focused on Peter and his ministry to the Jewish communities, as the Jews were to receive the gospel first. The second half of the book shifts to Paul and his ministry to the Gentiles, which brings up questions about how the Gentiles should respond to the gospel.

Themes

1. *The Promise and power of the Holy Spirit.*
2. *Power demonstrations leading to the Church growing.*
3. *Jesus' resurrection from the dead.*
4. *Being Jesus' witness to the nations.*
5. *Making disciples.*
6. *Persecution and pressures - mostly from Jews.*
7. *No fear of persecution or martyrdom.*
8. *Jewish transition to Messianic Judaism.*
9. *The gospel goes to the Jews first and then to the Gentiles.*

It is helpful to understand that Acts covers around thirty years of early Church history. At one point, I studied different resources to figure out what year each chapter was happening. Luke references many religious and secular events, places, and people, so there are confident estimates on Acts' timeline. I added this time frame to my book overview, and as I read different chapters in Acts, I knew about what year it was happening.

GENERAL BOOK OUTLINE

I usually make my first outline layer into 2-4 large sections. When I read Acts, I see two large sections—one focused on Peter and another focused on Paul. I titled both sections to summarize what I understand to be happening. The first section seems focused on the outpouring of the Holy Spirit, His impact in the early Church, and then the spreading of the gospel to the Jews specifically. The second half seems focused on Paul and his ministry to the Gentiles on his missionary journeys.

1. *The outpouring of the Spirit and the gospel to the Jews (1-12)*
2. *Paul takes the gospel to the Gentiles (13-28)*

My second outline layer breaks these larger sections into smaller ones based on themes or stories that fit together. In my reading, the first section is broken up into at least two smaller sections. The first five chapters are focused on the Holy Spirit and the Church in Jerusalem, and chapters 6-12 shift the focus to the gospel going out of Jerusalem. The second large section of Acts is centered around Paul's three missionary journeys, so I sectioned it off according to those trips.

1. *The outpouring of the Spirit and the gospel to the Jews (1-12)*
   i. *Early Church established (1-5)*
   ii. *Persecution takes the gospel to all of Israel (6-12)*
2. *Paul takes the gospel to the Gentiles (12-28)*
   i. *Paul's 1st missionary journey - sent from Antioch (13-14)*
   ii. *Paul's 2nd missionary journey - sent from Antioch (15-18:22)*
   iii. *Paul's 3rd missionary journey (18:23-21:26)*
   iv. *Paul imprisoned (21:27-28:31)*

WEEKLY ASSIGNMENT

You can do this! The Holy Spirit is with you to help you go deep in the Word and understand the things that He's written. Take it one step at a time and know that you'll grow in this depth of study as you practice it. Resist the lie that you can't understand or do an in-depth study like this and resist the temptation to be lazy in Bible study and say that this is too much work. You were made to go deep in the Word and have clarity! Every book of the Bible is available to you to understand if you give it time, and the Church needs you to encounter Jesus in your books and bring clarity to others! If you feel like you've been too casual about Bible study or have given up on the amount of time you can give it to the Word, take some time today to respond to God in any way that seems appropriate.

This week, begin your book study on a book of the Bible that is relevant to the truths you are seeking in this season. You will have three weeks to work on this book study. I suggest choosing a book that is under ten chapters long for your first time to make it easier. You will have three weeks to finish the book study assignments from this chapter and the next. Refer to the instructions in this chapter and research the book's background, read the book through several times, and create a general outline. In the following two weeks, you'll create a more detailed outline and write some personal commentary, so wherever you type out your information, format it in such a way that you can add to it each week.

26

BOOK STUDY PART TWO

▎ PERSONAL TESTIMONY

I am always significantly impacted and grow in understanding when I study a book of the Bible, but when I first started studying, I didn't enjoy it, and it intimidated me. In my early twenties, I read the Bible as best I could, but I didn't know how to go deeper, and I didn't feel confident in using the Bible resources that were available to me. The amount of history in the Bible overwhelmed me, and I didn't know where to start. In my life, studying and reading weren't even things I enjoyed doing.

I began Bible school when I was twenty-three, and I felt the same hindrances to Bible study going into my first year. The classes and teachers were excellent, but what really helped me grow in confidence in Bible study was the simple assignments that required me to take the extra effort to dig into the background of a book and create a simple outline. As I did this, I became more familiar with Bible resources and felt confident that I could learn Biblical history little by little.

One book that I had never understood, but desired to, was the book of Isaiah. Because of feeling intimidated and unequipped, I never would have studied the book by myself. In school, I took a class on Isaiah, and our assignment was to read the entire book several times and outline the whole thing.

The outlining process took a lot of diligence and time, but my heart came alive as I began to understand God's heart and message in Isaiah concerning the promised Son of David and the future glory of Jerusalem. Once I saw how Isaiah strategically built on his central themes section by section and understood his historical timeline, all the other minor details made more sense. That study laid the foundation for me so that each time I go back to the book, I can build on the clarity and understanding that I already have. One other benefit of Isaiah's class and assignments was that I felt bolder and more empowered to tackle any book of the Bible moving forward.

Another book study that impacted me was the book of Revelation. Like Isaiah, Revelation seemed like it was off-limits because of its size and my lack of familiarity with it. I read, meditated on, and studied the book for over a year as my weekly Bible study. As a result, I saw the beauty, mercy, and zealous love of God in the book. What was once a scary mystery to me became a place of encountering the Lamb of God in clarity.

I've outlined and written brief commentaries on many books, usually for a few months at a time. For Revelation, I created a verse-by-verse outline and wrote an extensive commentary for most verses. I didn't plan on commenting on most verses, and I didn't plan on writing so much, but the book pulled me in. There was so much content, and my heart was overflowing and discovering God. One phrase would move me at times, and I would meditate on it for days with a tender heart. At other times, a Bible commentary would clarify a chapter, and I would process my understanding in my writing. My outline and personal commentary became my journal with God for that year.

DEEPER LAYERS OF BOOK STUDY

In the previous chapter, I discussed how to begin a book study by researching its background, reading it several times, and creating a personal outline. You can choose to go as deep as you want in each one of these categories. This section will discuss the subsequent layers of book study, including more outlining layers and writing a personal commentary on sections or individual verses.

BOOK OUTLINE

To review, the first layer of outlining breaks a book into large sections. As a general idea, there may be two to four large sections in a book. I break Ephesians (1-3, 4-6) and Acts (1-12, 13-28) down into two sections. The second layer breaks these larger sections into smaller ones. Depending on the size of the book you want to study, these sections may be a few Bible chapters long or the size of one Bible chapter.

The next step is to add more complex layers to your outline and title each section. The number of outline layers will depend on how long the book is and how in-depth you want to break it down. Each layer will break the smaller sections based on subpoints. Each layer is worth the extra effort.

1. **Third outline layer** – Take the sections that are one or more Bible chapters long and divide them into smaller sections. For a shorter book, these sections will be half a chapter-long or shorter. In a longer book, these sections might be one or two chapters long. In my book of Acts example, Acts 1-5 is broken into four smaller sections around one chapter in size (1-2, 3, 4:1-33, 4:34-5:42).

2. **Fourth outline layer** – These small sections will be several verses long in a shorter book and would be a good place to stop to begin to write your commentary. In a longer book, these sections are several verses to half a chapter in size. In my book of Acts example, Acts 1-2 is broken into six sections (1:1-11, 1:12-26, 2:1-4, 2:5-13, 2:14-40, 2:41-47).

3. **Fifth outline layer** – These small sections will be around one or two verses long. In my Acts example, 1:1-11 is broken down into three sections (1:1-3, 4-8, 9-11).

4. **Title each section** – Write a few words or a short sentence to title each section you make. The purpose of the title is to summarize the main point of the section in your own words.

PERSONAL COMMENTARY

After doing all the work of reading, outlining, and titling a book or a section of a book, it's time to study individual passages and write down your study results. A personal commentary is a collection of your thoughts, meditations, observations, topical studies, and word studies from individual verses. You can do as much or as little writing as you want. So you could write a sentence in one section and pages in another.

A titled outline is an optimal and very natural place to begin studying smaller sections or individual verses. The outlining process brings you into the bigger picture of a book and the flow of thought from one section to the next, so studying smaller units and writing your ideas will be a natural next step. I type out my outlines on my laptop and then write all of my studies in the outline in paragraphs.

This format gives me the ability to have all of my content in one place so that I can reference material and build on it each day. I still reference my old outlines and commentaries when preparing for Bible teachings or Bible studies. Below is a list of things I include in my writing.

1. **Thoughts** – I write down all my initial thoughts, observations, and questions as a way of processing the Bible verses.

2. **Bible verses** – If other verses connect to the verses I'm studying, I copy and paste them into my commentary. There are no rules; at times, I have one or two pages of verses typed in just for fun.

3. **Topical studies** – When I find a topic in a verse to study in more depth, I research the topic and compile the results in my commentary. While reading Acts, I noticed there were many supernatural stories. One day, I spent an entire study time skimming through the book to find and type out every event. I copied every story into my commentary and then wrote a sentence summary about each event.

4. **Word studies** – When I find a word that I want to understand better, I do a word study and compile all of my findings in my commentary. This includes researching the word in the original language and looking at every verse that uses that word. Example words from Acts are hope, resurrection, filled with Spirit, witness, tongues, and kingdom.

5. **Commentaries** – When I'm at a stopping point in my studies on a verse or don't know what the verse is talking about, I read commentaries. Commentaries are an excellent resource in that they offer several interpretations, explain their thought process, give historical context, and reference Bible verses for further study. I write down any helpful information.

You can access multiple commentaries on most Bible study websites. If you go to studylight.org, click on "Bible Study Tools" and then select "Commentaries." Another helpful website is Biblehub.com, which allows you to see multiple commentaries side by side. All you have to do is type in your verse and click the "comment" tab at the top, and all the commentary on your verse will pull up. I encourage you to read as many commentaries on your verses as you find helpful.

If you plan to study a book in-depth for a few months, I recommend buying a hard copy commentary to track with during your study. To go deep into the big picture of a book without studying individual verses, I recommend a simpler commentary series such as *The Bible Speaks today* by Intervarsity Press. It will give you a good background, insight into the book's flow, and commentary on sections of the book. It is very understandable for beginner Bible students.

A more extensive commentary will have verse by verse commentary with Greek and Hebrew word studies and more detailed explanations of interpretations. These commentaries are constructive if you are ready to read a lot of information and if you can decide which information to focus on. For example, an extensive commentary series I purchase for verse-by-verse book studies is the *Baker Exegetical Commentary on the New Testament*.

6. **Meditations** – Bible study leads to Bible meditation. When a verse moves my heart, I meditate on it and journal in my study notes. My meditations could include writing down prayers from the truth of the verse.

EXAMPLE OUTLINES

Don't be intimidated by this outline or the personal commentary in the next section. This took some time to read through Acts and a few times of changing the outline. Also, I made it look as good as I could to be in a book. Remember, there are no rules as to how your outline should look, and you can adjust the outline as many times as you want. The process of outlining is what benefits you the most, not having it "perfect."

#1 OUTLINE LAYER

1. *The outpouring of the Spirit and the gospel to the Jews (1-12)*
2. *Paul Takes the Gospel to the Gentiles (13-28)*

#2 OUTLINE LAYER (THE NEW LAYER IS BOLDED)

1. *The outpouring of the Spirit and the gospel to the Jews (1-12)*
   a. ***Early Church Established (1-5)***
   b. ***Persecution Takes the Gospel to All of Israel (6-12)***

2. *Paul takes the gospel to the Gentiles (13-28)*
   a. ***Paul's 1ˢᵗ Missionary Journey – Sent from Antioch (13-14)***
   b. ***Paul's 2ⁿᵈ Missionary Journey – Sent from Antioch (15-18:22)***

    c. *Paul's 3ʳᵈ Missionary Journey – (18:23-21:26)*

    d. *Paul Imprisoned (21:27-28:31)*

#3 OUTLINE LAYER (THE NEW LAYER IS BOLDED)

1. *The outpouring of the Spirit and the gospel to the Jews (1-12)*
   a. *Early Church Established (1-5)*
      i. **The Outpouring of the Spirit (1-2)**
      ii. **Healing and Preaching at the Temple (3)**
      iii. **Jewish Leadership Confronted with Power – 1ˢᵗ Time (4:1-33)**
      iv. **Fear of God Falls on the Church – 2ⁿᵈ Time Jewish Leadership Confronted (4:34-5:42)**

2. *Persecution takes the gospel to All of Israel (6-12)*
      i. **Stephen Killed – 3ʳᵈ Time Jewish Leadership Confronted (6-7)**
      ii. **The Gospel Goes to Judea and Samaria – Philip the Evangelist (8)**
      iii. **Saul Converted and Commissioned to the Gentiles (9)**
      iv. **Peter Brings the Gospel to the Gentiles – Cornelius (10)**
      v. **Apostles Bless the Gentile Conversions - Antioch Highlighted (11)**
      vi. **Peter Imprisoned and Herod Killed – Paul Highlighted (12)**

#4 OUTLINE LAYER (THE NEW LAYER IS BOLDED)

1. *The Outpouring of the Spirit and the Gospel to the Jews (1-12)*
   a. *Early Church Established (1-5)*
   i. *The Outpouring of the Spirit (1-2)*
      1. **Jesus' Resurrected Ministry (1:1-11)**
      2. **Apostolic Leadership Established (1:12-26)**
      3. **Corporate Prayer and Pentecost (2:1-4)**
      4. **Tongues Amaze Jerusalem (2:5-13)**
      5. **Peter's 1ˢᵗ Prophetic Sermon (2:14-40)**
      6. **First Wave of Salvation (2:41-47)**
   ii. *Healing and Preaching at the Temple (3)*

    1. Lame Man Healed (3:1-11)

    2. Peter's 2ⁿᵈ Prophetic Sermon (3:12-26)

  iii. Jewish Leadership Confronted with Power – 1st Time (4:1-33)

    1. Peter and John Imprisoned (4:1-22)

    2. 2ⁿᵈ Outpouring of the Spirit – Praying Church (4:23-33)

  iv. Fear of God Falls on the Church – 2ⁿᵈ Time Jewish Leadership Confronted (4:34-5:42)

    1. Radical Christian Giving (4:34-37)

    2. Ananias and Sapphira Judged (5:1-11)

    3. Healing Revival on the Streets (5:12-16)

    4. Apostles Imprisoned (5:17-40)

#5 OUTLINE LAYER (NEW LAYER BOLDED)

1. *The Outpouring of the Spirit and the Gospel to the Jews (1-12)*

  a. Early Church Established (1-5)

  i. The Outpouring of the Spirit (1-2)

    1. Jesus' Resurrected Ministry (1:1-11)

    a. Jesus' 40 days of teaching (1:1-3)

    b. Jesus Promises the Spirit (1:4-8)

    c. Jesus Ascends in the Clouds (1:9-11)

▌EXAMPLE PERSONAL COMMENTARY

This section includes how I organize my thoughts and studies in a book study. At the end, I included a commentary quotation and extra information from an online article to show how you can incorporate Bible resources.

1. Jesus' Resurrected Ministry (1:1-11)

After His resurrection, Jesus was with His disciples for forty days before He ascended into heaven. During this time, He spoke to them about His kingdom and told them to wait and pray in Jerusalem until He poured out the Holy Spirit. The disciples would end up praying for ten days before the Spirit was released. There was a fifty-day gap between Jesus' resurrection and the outpouring of the Spirit, which came during the Jewish feast of Pentecost.

This section of Acts introduces the Spirit's outpouringandthecommandment to take His power to the nations. These two statements unfold through the entire book of Acts. Jesus also highlights these two things before His ascension to heaven.

"Acts begins with a short prologue that connects the book to Luke's Gospel and introduces the key themes of Acts: (1) Jesus is alive and functioning at God's right hand; (2) the promised Spirit will come and enable the new mission in fulfillment of divine promise; (3) the message of the kingdom is to go out into all the world, starting from Jerusalem."[1]

Jesus' 40 days of teaching (1:1-3)

The former account to Theophilus *- Luke was writing to Theophilus, who was possibly a Roman Official who was a follower of Jesus or was interested in faith in Jesus. The former account is the book of Luke. Acts is part two of Luke's account. Acts 1 is similar to Luke 24 and then transitions into the rest of the early Church's story. In Acts 1, Luke includes proof that Jesus was seen by many for forty days and taught about His kingdom during that time.*

Jesus began to do and teach *- What Jesus began to do in the earthly ministry will be continued through His people after His ascension to the Father. He will continue to teach and do works of power through His Church. Jesus taught on the kingdom of God and demonstrated the kingdom of God with power. Jesus combined doing the works of the kingdom with teaching on the kingdom.*

Jesus presented Himself alive *- Jesus purposefully presented Himself to the Apostles and disciples to prove His resurrection and leave credible eyewitnesses.*

---

[1] Darrell L. Bock. *Acts*. Baker's Exegetical Commentary on the New Testament (Grand Rapids, MI: Baker Academic, 2007), 49.

Jesus appeared sequentially to many people over forty days.[2] *At one point, Jesus was seen by 500 people as proof of His resurrection. What was it like to see the resurrected Lord walking and talking and eating?*

1. *Mary Magdalene at the tomb (John 20:11-17)*
2. *The women (Matthew 28:9-10)*
3. *Peter (Luke 24:34)*
4. *Two disciples (Luke 24:13-35; Mark 16:12-13)*
5. *The eleven apostles, except Thomas, and those with them (Luke 24:36)*
6. *The eleven with Thomas (John 20:26-29)*
7. *Seven disciples at the Sea of Tiberias (John 21:1-23)*
8. *Disciples and a possible large gathering of 500 in Galilee (1 Corinthians 15:6; Matthew 28:16-18)*
9. *James, Jesus' brother (1 Corinthians 15:7)*
10. *Disciples before His ascension (Luke 24:49-53)*

Jesus spoke about the kingdom of God - *Jesus continued His teaching ministry during the forty days, and one of His topics was the kingdom of God. We don't know everything He said about the kingdom, but what He said caused the disciples to ask if it was time to restore the kingdom to Israel.*[3] *The topic of God's kingdom is related to His promises for the nation of Israel. Jesus is the king of the Jews, and He will return as the Messiah who restores all things. He will restore all things as a king in Jerusalem.*

The kingdom of God was Jesus' primary topic during His life. His kingdom is mentioned eight times in Acts (1:3, 6; 8:12; 14:22; 19:8; 20:25; 28:23; 28:31).

But when they believed Philip as he preached the things concerning the kingdom of God and the name of Jesus Christ, both men and women were baptized.—Acts 8:12

---

[2]   Dr. Elizabeth Mitchell, "The Sequence of Christ's Post-Resurrection Appearances," *Answers in Depth*, March 21, 2012. (https://answersingenesis.org/jesus/ resurrection/the-sequence-of-christs- post-resurrection-appearances/)

[3]   Acts 1:6.

So when they had appointed him a day, many came to him at his lodging, to whom he explained and solemnly testified of the kingdom of God, persuading them concerning Jesus from both the Law of Moses and the Prophets, from morning till evening.—Acts 28:23

Jesus, teach me about the kingdom of God. Show me what you talked about in the gospels. Show me what you talked about with the disciples before Your ascension. Show me what they knew about the kingdom in Acts and the New Testament letters. I want to know about You as King, and I want to know about Your kingdom. I want to persuade people about the kingdom as Paul did. I want to do miracles as a testimony of the kingdom like Philip did. Bring me into a greater paradigm and reality of living in Your kingdom.

OVERCOME INTIMIDATION

As you read this chapter and continue in your Bible study assignments, be encouraged that you can have an organized in-depth Bible study and love it. Some parts of the process may take more time or energy than you are used to, but it will become second nature to you if you take it step by step. The Bible study assignments will give you an opportunity to grow in these specific study approaches but continue to look at these Bible study chapters and grow in your study skills after this module.

If you feel overwhelmed or intimidated by in-depth study and struggle with thoughts that it isn't for you, now is the time to break agreement with lies and move into the things God has for you. You can understand entire books of the Bible! Break off the spirit of intimidation. You can know the Word and discover God in any book that you desire. You have the ability to understand Genesis, Isaiah, Song of Songs, Matthew, Romans, Revelation, and any other book of the Bible. There's a line to cross in your heart as to whether you believe you can and should go deep in Bible understanding, and I encourage you to step over that line today.

▌WEEKLY ASSIGNMENT

The process of reading, researching, outlining, and commenting can be done to any level that you desire for any book. You could do a surface-level study of a book and get a lot out of it, or you could take more time and get even more out of it. Either way is fine. If you don't want to study an entire book and have one section you want to focus on, read the entire book and do one or two layers of outline for the book. Then do several outlining layers and write a commentary on the one chapter you want as your focus.

This week, apply the instructions from this chapter and add more outlining layers (2-3 more layers) to the outline you created last week. Next week, write your commentary on one section of verses (about 5-10 verses) that are the most relevant to you. This includes writing thoughts on the overall section and then verse by verse commentary. Remember, this isn't an assignment for a grade, this is a practical way to get you into the truths you want to impact you in this season. Resist the temptation to "just get it done." Instead, pour yourself into this study and encounter God.

DISCIPLESHIP MEETING GUIDE
MODULE 6: BIBLE STUDY – CHAPTERS 25 & 26

MEETING FOCUS:

The purpose of this meeting is to discuss your Book Study assignment and continue praying through your heart issue.

DISCUSSION QUESTIONS (IN ORDER OF IMPORTANCE):

1. *Heart Issue:*
   a. Share how your heart issue has been going since the last meeting. Take time together to ask God for more clarity concerning the current heart issue or ask Him to highlight more things to pray through during this meeting. Use the simple deliverance prayer steps from the last module.

2. *Chapter Questions:*
   a. Chapter 25 & 26 – Discuss any journaled thoughts and questions from the chapters. Do you have the vision to go deep in Bible study? Does in-depth Bible study intimidate you?
   b. Book Study Assignment – In-depth, discuss how the Book Study is going for you and what you are learning about your book of the Bible.

3. *Spiritual Pursuits:*
   a. Practically, how is your prayer schedule going? How many days have you walked out your prayer schedule? Do you need to make small changes to your schedule? How are your daily prayer times going, and how is God impacting you through them?

4. Briefly review the assignments for the next two weeks together.

MEETING NOTES:

_____

_____

_____

_____

_____

_____

_____

_____

_____

_____

_____

_____

27

WORD STUDIES & INTERPRETATION

THE BIBLE FUELS PRAYER

The Bible is the most powerful thing God has given to anchor and fuel our hearts. God wants His Word to be the center of our relationship with Him and for every prayer expression to flow out of it. When we make the Bible the centerpiece of our life in God, His words become like logs that sustain the bonfire of prayer in our hearts.

Reading and meditating on the Bible imparts life to us in the form of faith, conviction, and informed conversation with God. The Word renews our faith and inspires us with promises of our inheritance in God. It sensitizes and aligns our conscience to God's standards of love and purity. Lastly, the Word directs and informs our conversation with God in that what He stirs in us during our Bible times becomes the primary thing He is doing in our hearts. God directs our conversations with Him based on what He leads us to dive into in the Word, and He informs our prayer conversation with the content of His Word.

I believe that a deep pursuit of God in His Word is central to growing in a life of prayer. I find that my prayer life (worship, praying in tongues, intercession, etc.) rises or falls depending on my level of engagement with God in His Word during any given week. If I don't have regular times with Him in the Word during a week, but I'm still having focused prayer and worship times, I feel slightly disoriented in my heart and sense a lack of intimate connection with God. My faith decreases, and my conscience is weakened. If I give Him focused time in the Word and open my heart to His truth, I feel aligned in my convictions, strengthened with faith in His promises, and my conversation with Him overflows with Biblical clarity.

BIBLE-CENTERED FRIENDSHIPS

Deep and meaningful friendships are based on the place of pursuing God together. One of the ways we seek Him as friends is to go deep in the Word together. If the main thing God is doing in us revolves around what we're reading and meditating on, the most meaningful thing we could share with our friends is what God is speaking to us through the Word.

God created the human heart to function and thrive in the context of community. He designed us to be known and to know others in an intentional and meaningful way. We were created to overflow in love for people in our families and our friendships; to have intimacy without shame, to be ourselves and loved in our weakness, to be encouraged to grow at a pace faster than what we would be able to alone. To have a godly and Biblical community, there has to be a foundation that centers our relationships, and for believers, that is the Bible.

The Word is longing to find a home in our hearts, but also in our friendships. God designed us to thrive in spiritual truth and life, and we only find that kind of life in interacting with the Holy Spirit in conversation with the Bible. In the same vein, our friendships can only have unique life and truth flowing to each relationship if the Word is at the center. It is crucial to find friends that long for that same truth and life as we do.

How does this look? Discuss, digest, talk through, weep, and celebrate what each other is studying and talking to the Lord about from the Word. Share the truths that have impacted you and give language to what God is saying to you in the Bible. In these times of sharing, you and your friends will begin to receive faith, conviction, and clarity from the Holy Spirit, you'll speak truth to one another. Whenever I do this with my family and friends, my revelation increases while speaking, and they add revelation spontaneously or from an understanding they've already had. At times, God's presence rests on us and we enter into an encounter with God together. When this happens, we respond to Him in prayer, thanksgiving, or repentance.

PRACTICAL RESPONSE

There are two practical responses to this exhortation on friendships. The first response is to consider focusing a lot of your conversation time with friends around what you're reading in the Bible and what God is speaking to you through it. Help shape your friendship culture by talking to your friends and asking if they'd like to make the Word a central part of your time together. Bring your Bible to hang-outs and ask each person to share what God is doing in their heart. This is challenging to do if you or your friends aren't really reading the Bible, but if you all agree to the vision of Bible-centered friendship, you can quickly grow in Bible reading and conversation.

If you're married, make what God is doing in you and your spouse in the Word the central focus of your relationship and conversation. If you have children, bring them into this Bible culture by having them read their age-appropriate Bible with you every day and make it a part of your dinner conversations. Those of you who have siblings and parents who love Jesus, ask them if they would like to make Jesus and the Bible a regular part of the family relationship.

WORD STUDIES

A word study is the study of an individual word's meaning in a Bible verse. They are done by researching the meaning of words in their original language and comparing them in other verses. Hebrew is the original language for Old Testament words, and Greek is the original language for New Testament words. Word studies are very easy, and everyone who has access to Bible resources can do them well.

Before moving on, I want to be clear that we can interpret the Bible with clarity and depth without knowing the meaning of words in their original language. Sometimes, newer Bible students assume that knowing the true meaning of a word is always the way to understand a verse fully. But meditation, understanding the flow of thought, and knowing the original audience are the most essential interpretation elements. In some verses, word studies can bring much-needed insight, and in other verses, they only add a little flavor or meaning to the translated word.

Word studies are a natural fit and support to topical and book studies. When you study a topic, you will most likely have keywords you're searching out. These keywords can turn into word studies to add more depth of understanding.

An example word study within a topical study is the word "hope." While researching the topic of what hope is and what we're to hope in, it would make sense to understand the Hebrew or Greek meaning of the word. You might find more than one Hebrew or Greek word for the English word hope, which might impact how you understand verses on hope.

When doing a book study, you will naturally want to do word studies when writing a commentary on individual verses. When you get to a word that interests you or limits your understanding of a verse, do a word study. Based on what you discover in the study, fill your commentary with your findings.

HOW TO DO WORD STUDIES

There are two parts to doing a word study. The first part is to research the meaning of the word in the original language. The second part is to compare every verse that uses the word to understand the different contexts in which it's used. To research the Hebrew and Greek meanings, go to a Bible study website with a Bible search engine and Bible resources like commentaries and dictionaries. The resource that is needed for word studies is called an Interlinear Study Bible. This resource will show you the Bible in your language next to the Bible in the Greek or Hebrew language so you can easily see what words you're researching.

1. Go to www.studylight.org and click on the "Language Tools" tab on the top. Then select the "Hebrew" tab if you need an Old Testament verse or select the "Greek" tab for New Testament verses. Next, click on the book and chapter of the Bible you need and find your specific verse.

2. At this point, you should see every Bible verse of the chapter you selected in your language with Greek or Hebrew words above most of your words. The Greek or Hebrew words correspond to the word in your translation.

3. The numbers above the words are assigned to each Greek and Hebrew word based on a Bible resource called *The Strong's Concordance.*

4. Click the word that you want to study, and all its information will show up. The information will include summarized meanings of the word, what other words it comes from or is similar to, and a list of every verse that contains the word. The list of verses is necessary for the second part of a word study, which is to read all the verses containing the word. When you read every verse, you can see the different contexts in which your word is being used.

5. Click on each listed book of the Bible, and you will see every verse that uses your word. Click on every book and read every verse. Write down your observations about how the word was used or the context in which it was used. Also, write down anything you learn from the verses or themes you see. In doing this, your word study could blossom into an interesting topical study that will make the word come alive!

EXAMPLE WORD STUDY

My word study is on the New Testament Greek word for "hope." The verses that I'm starting my research in are Romans 8:24-25, "*For we were saved in this hope, but hope that is seen is not hope; for why does one still hope for what he sees? But if we hope for what we do not see, we eagerly wait for it with perseverance.*" The first step is to look at Romans 8:24-25 in the Interlinear Bible to get information on the Greek word. The second step is to compare all the verses in which it is used. The third step is to summarize the findings and write down my thoughts on the meaning and use of the word.

> *The Greek word for hope is "elpis." The Strong's Concordance number is #1680.[1] It comes from the Greek word "elpo," which means to anticipate something with pleasure. Thayer's definition says it's a, "Joyful and confident expectation of eternal salvation." This word is used fourteen times in Romans, more than any other book in the New Testament. It is used fifty-four times in the New Testament. In almost every verse, it is translated as "hope."*

> *Elpis is a noun and not a verb. When Paul or others used this word, they talked about hope as an object or referred to our faith in the future as an object or a thing. We have hope, or we hope in something. Most of the time, the book of Romans uses this noun form.*

> *"Men and Brethren, I am a Pharisee, the son of a Pharisee: concerning the hope and resurrection of the dead I am being judged."—Acts 23:6*

---

[1] Strong's Greek #1680 - https://www.studylight.org/lexicons/eng/greek/1680.html

Who contrary to hope, in hope believed, so that he became the father of many nations.—Romans 4:18

Elpizō (Strong's #1679) is the verb form of elpís.[2] The verb is used thirty-six times in the New Testament. Out of the three times the verb is used in Romans, Romans 8:25 is one of them. In these verses, hope is an action in the heart of the believer. This word is also translated as "trust" and "expect" in some versions. Some versions say to "set" or "fix" our hope on God.

For to this end we both labor and suffer reproach, because we trust in the living God, who is the Savior of all men, especially of those who believe.
—1 Timothy 4:10

Command those who are rich in this present age not to be haughty, nor to trust in uncertain riches but in the living God, who gives us richly all things to enjoy.—1 Timothy 6:17

Therefore gird up the loins of your mind, be sober, and rest your hope fully upon the grace that is to be brought to you at the revelation of Jesus Christ.
—1 Peter 1:13

My summary understanding is that our hope is set on an object or an event, and it is something we engage within our thoughts, emotions, and will. Hope is a joyful emotion related to something in the future that can increase as an experience. The anticipation and expectation of the future bring pleasure now. Hope is confidence, expectation, and trust in something or someone. We can move our hearts to trust in or hope in God. We have to determine what we put our internal trust and hope in because it is something we set or fix our hearts on. In Roman 8:24-25, the hope is in our future resurrected body and restored earth. Hoping in these things will produce joyful anticipation in our thoughts and emotions and cause us to "eagerly wait for it with perseverance." The clearer the future or the object of hope, the more joy and excitement we will have in the waiting.

---

2   Strong's Greek #1679 - https://www.studylight.org/lexicons/eng/greek/1679.html

After looking at the context of the verses that talk about hope, I would do some further studies on the broader topic of hope. First, I would want to research all the godly and ungodly things in the Old and New Testament verses that people have hoped in. After that study, I would want to investigate the present-tense effect of hope in the lives of God's people in the Bible.

INTERPRETATION PRINCIPLES

ORIGINAL MEANING

The main goal in interpreting Bible verses is to discover what God and the author were trying to communicate to the original hearers in their day and life context. Interpretation is understanding what the original message was, and application is understanding how that interpretation applies to your life context. Once you have a sense of the verse's interpretation, you can apply the timeless truth or principle to your life.

PLAIN-SENSE MEANING

The Bible is meant to be read and understood in a literal way unless there are clear stories with one main point, analogies, or symbols that need to be further understood. When a verse seems literal, take the literal or the plain sense meaning of the verse as your interpretation. If you realize you're reading an analogy, a parable, or something with symbols, understand that your interpretation may not be literal. In saying that, many of these verses do have a plain sense or a straightforward meaning that most people can understand.

You don't have to "read between the lines" or find a hidden spiritual meaning to a verse to find the true meaning or for it to qualify as a revelation from God. Read things in a literal way to develop your interpretation of verses. As you do this, God will give you deeper meanings, and He'll help you understand His heart behind His words, but it will still fit within the meaning of the verses. My suggestion is if your "deeper meaning" interpretation doesn't line up with other Bible verses, and if your friends and leaders don't see your interpretation, it probably isn't accurate, or it needs further development.

HISTORICAL-CULTURAL CONTEXT

What does historical-cultural context mean in Bible interpretation? It refers to understanding some of the histories of the people, places, and events surrounding the time frame of a book of the Bible. It also refers to understanding the cultural values and practices of the author and original readers. The history and the culture set the scene or the background for your reading. If the goal of interpretation is to understand the original message to the original hearers, then we must know what their worlds looked like.

For example, it is beneficial to understand some possible cultural practices of Corinth when reading 1 Corinthians 11 and the topic of head coverings. In the city of Corinth, head coverings and hair length for men and women were significant. They communicated cultural status and values in a completely different way than they do in American culture. To interpret this chapter without cultural understanding leads to wrong conclusions.

A little information will help you significantly, but you can study as much as you want about the history and culture behind books of the Bible, and you would reap even more understanding.

BOOK CONTEXT

Book context refers to understanding individual verses in light of the big picture message of the surrounding verses, the chapter around it, and even the entire book. Individual verses or words make the most sense when understood within the larger message that is being presented. When verses are not interpreted in context to the book and surrounding verses, they can be misunderstood and misinterpreted. Find the main context by looking at the few verses surrounding your main verse, then work your way out from there and find the larger context of the chapter and then the book. Each layer will add context to the verse you're trying to interpret.

Book context also refers to understanding the style or genre of the book or verses being read. The main genres in the Bible are narrative, law, prophetic, poetic, wisdom, Gospels, and letters. Each genre has its own way of communicating and developing main points, and this affects how we are supposed to read and interpret. Having a simple understanding of the genre will further equip you to develop an interpretation. You can pursue more information on a book's style and genre by researching its background and using commentaries.

COMPARE TO THE BIBLE

Compare your understanding and interpretation of an individual verse to the rest of the Bible to get a fuller truth and find contradictions in your interpretation. The verse you're studying may have a part of the truth on a topic, but other verses may have other parts of the truth that are needed to bring together a fuller picture of the topic. Your interpretation should never contradict other Bible verses. If it seems to contradict other verses, you probably don't have a true understanding of the verse, or you need to wrestle with a few Bible verses and see how they work together.

For example, within the topic of women in church leadership, there are several verses that seem to contradict each other. Some verses indicate restrictions on women ministering to people, while other verses describe women ministering without limitation. When one of these verses is not compared to other verses, the interpretation is limited and can be filled with error. When these verses are viewed together, a fuller message comes to the surface, changes how we interpret each individual verse, and explains the seeming contradictions.

▋ WEEKLY ASSIGNMENT

Your first assignment this week is to think and pray about how you can apply your Bible study tools in your weekly times with God moving forward. Each module is meant to equip you in your times with God, so how can you apply Bible study in your prayer schedule? Write down what you want to read or study in the Bible for the next 1-2 months, what your approach is going to be (general reading, topical study, book study), a simple action plan, and when you'll study in your prayer schedule.

Your second assignment this week is to do a word study from a verse you did a personal commentary on during the last two weeks of the book study assignment. I encourage you to pick a word that would help you understand a verse or a word that seems significant to you. Follow the directions from this chapter and write your findings in your commentary.

DISCIPLESHIP MEETING GUIDE
MODULE 6: BIBLE STUDY – CHAPTER 27

MEETING FOCUS:

The purpose of this meeting is to discuss your Book Study and Word Study assignments and continue praying through your heart issue.

DISCUSSION QUESTIONS (IN ORDER OF IMPORTANCE):

1. *Heart Issue:*
   a. Share how your heart issue has been going since the last meeting. Take time together to ask God for more clarity concerning the current heart issue or ask Him to highlight more things to pray through during this meeting. Use the simple deliverance prayer steps from the last module.

2. *Chapter Questions:*
   a. Chapter 27 - Discuss your journaled thoughts and questions from the chapter. What are your thoughts on the Bible-centered friendships section?
   b. Study assignments - In-depth, discuss what you wrote in your personal commentary in the Book Study. Also, share about your Word Study assignment. Share how both assignments impacted you.

3. *Spiritual pursuits:*
   a. Together, create a schedule and plan for including the new Bible study tools into your prayer schedule. Decide what you will read or study next, what approach you'll take, and if you need to make changes to your prayer schedule.

4. Briefly review the assignments for the next two weeks together. This is not necessary if you are having a group gathering to introduce the next module topic.

MEETING NOTES:

THRONE ROOM

MODULE INTRODUCTION

The purpose of this module is to equip you to access your position in God's throne room and behold God's beauty with your spiritual eyes (imagination). The first chapter will focus on your access and position as a priest in God's throne room, while the following three chapters will walk you through the throne room descriptions from Revelation 4. Through the process of meditating on His throne room, God will train your mind to see Him every time you talk or sing to Him. Your conversations with Him will become more tangible, and your faith in the power of prayer will increase.

Throughout this module, I'll frequently reference the idea of beholding or gazing at God's beauty. Beholding God or gazing on God means meditating on the Biblical descriptions of God's physical presence in His throne room and looking at Him with your spiritual eyes. Gazing on God means we enter into the beautiful throne room scene with our spiritual eyes and then stay there with a gazing posture like the living creatures with all eyes all over their bodies. I like the words beholding and gazing because they have the sense of looking and focusing on God's beauty in an attitude of wonder and holy fascination.

For your assignments, you will meditate on specific descriptions of God and His throne room from Revelation 4. Take the time to picture the descriptions in your prayer times and know that the Holy Spirit will help you paint the picture over time. As you meditate on the verses in the next chapters, go deep in what each description reveals about God, but give the most attention to entering into the actual images. Wait for the Spirit to bring you into an encounter with God. Revelation will come through Biblical ideas, but it will also come through multi- sensory (hearing, feeling, seeing, smelling) experiences through your spiritual senses, and then ideas and truths will flow from that place.

ASSIGNMENT OVERVIEW
MODULE 7 – THRONE ROOM

Continue to follow your prayer schedule and Spiritual Pursuits each week. During week 34 or 35, schedule one 30-minute group tongue time. In the prayer time, pick one throne room description and meditate on it together by praying in tongues, picturing the description, and taking turns praying out the truths of the description.

Week Thirty-two Assignments:

❑ Read Chapter 28 – "**Seated in God's Temple.**" Journal your thoughts and questions about the chapter.

❑ Read the throne room Bible chapters and briefly pray phrases of Revelation 4 during a prayer time this week.

❑ Fill out a new *Spiritual Pursuits Document*. The pursuits can stay the same or change but filling out the form helps you refocus and develop a rhythm of intentionality. Include your new Bible study plan while maintaining the other prayer expressions in your schedule.

Week Thirty-three Assignments:

❑ Read Chapter 29 – "**God's Throne and Glorious Colors.**" Journal your thoughts and questions about the chapter.

❑ In one prayer time, picture the descriptions from the chapter and journal your experience.

❑ **Meet with Discipleship Mentor.**

Week Thirty-four Assignments:

❑ Read Chapter 30 – "**God's Glory Storm.**" Journal your thoughts and questions about the chapter.

❑ In one prayer time, picture the descriptions from the chapter and journal your experience.

Week Thirty-five Assignments:

❑ Read Chapter 31 – "**Around God's Throne.**" Journal your thoughts and questions.

❑ In one prayer time, picture the descriptions from the chapter and journal your experience.

❑ Participate in one 30-minute group tongues time. Together, focus on one throne room description while praying in tongues and in your under- standing.

❑ **Meet with Discipleship Mentor.**

SPIRITUAL PURSUITS   DATE: _____

1. **Bible reading direction and plan**
   (Write down what you will read and when you will read it):

2. **Meditation verse** (Choose a verse that speaks truth into your heart issue):

3. **Sin/character issue from which to get freedom:**

4. **Lie from which to pursue deliverance:**

5. **Gifting to pursue** (Include simple ways you can pursue it):

7. **Weekly Prayer Schedule**—Write down your plan for the *specific times* you are committed to spending with God each day, and *what specifically you plan to do during those times*. Include what your study or meditation focus will be. Refer to the example schedule in Chapter Two. (e.g., Monday 6-6:30 am—Tongues, 6:30-7:30 am—Meditation on Song of Solomon 1:2)

Monday

Tuesday

Wednesday

Thursday

Friday

Saturday

28

SEATED IN GOD'S TEMPLE

MY TESTIMONY

In my early years, my prayer life was transformed as I learned to engage God as a Person with my spiritual eyes. The principle of interacting with God with my spiritual senses became foundational, and it became a fountain of encounter from which worship gushed out. As a fruit of consistently meditating on the throne room in Revelation 4, my imagination quickly pictures Him and engages with Him whenever I spend time with Him. When I close my eyes, I see, hear, and feel the whispers of that room and God's splendor as though I'm really there. This has been a powerful way to connect to Him as a real person, a helpful way to stay focused and engaged in my mind, and a place to experience awe and fascination with God. Most people struggle in prayer because of distracted thinking and because they don't have anything to focus their minds on. I've found that the prayer posture of gazing on God addresses the issue of a distracted mind and exercises more of our spiritual senses. Not only does it heal distraction, gazing on God supernaturally connects us to our heavenly position in Jesus and causes us to live from the throne room in every area of our lives.

SETTING OUR MINDS ON GOD

If then you were raised with Christ, seek those things which are above, where Christ is, sitting at the right hand of God. Set your mind on things above, not on things on the earth. For you died, and your life is hidden with Christ in God. When Christ who is our life appears, then you also will appear with Him in glory. Therefore put to death your members which are on the earth: fornication, uncleanness, passion, evil desire, and covetousness, which is idolatry.—Colossians 3:1-5

In Colossians 3, Paul calls believers to come into God's throne room to gaze on His beauty as a part of our inheritance in Christ. I love how he begins this chapter, "If then you were raised with Christ." If God raised our spirits with Christ into heaven, the logical response is to access and live from our position and experience in heaven. This passage screams of our identity in Christ and the benefits God has for us through His Son.

Initially, you might not see the throne room language in these verses, but Paul is clearly talking about the heavenly throne room. He uses different words to describe heaven, such as being "raised" with Christ, seeking those things which are "above," "where Christ is sitting at the right hand of God," and setting your mind on things "above" rather than the things on earth. Our spirits have access to heaven, but our members (bodies) are "on the earth." All these phrases are pointing to the throne room in heaven where Jesus and the Father are sitting.

PAUL'S INSIGHT

Paul invites us to enter the throne room in these verses and then tells us how to enter. He says to "set your mind on things above" as the pathway of spiritually accessing the throne room where God dwells. Paul is saying that believers can enter into and perceive the spiritual realm by setting their thoughts on God. We gaze on God and pursue experiences with Him in His throne room by setting our minds on Bible verses that describe Him and the throne room. Engaging our minds in Biblical meditation is a crucial spiritual principle!

What does it mean to set your mind on something? Setting your mind refers to choosing to think about a Biblical truth during meditation. You have to decide to focus your attention on God; otherwise, your mind will gravitate towards other things. Choosing to bring our thoughts into focus on God to experience Him, rather than focusing on the desires of the flesh, was one of Paul's main teaching points throughout his letters.[1] In context to the throne room, we set our minds by thinking about and praying about the Biblical descriptions of God's throne room.

The second aspect of setting our minds is to focus our thoughts on God's image. Our imaginations are from God, and they are our spiritual eyes with which we can behold God's faint image. In Ephesians 1, Paul calls them the "eyes of your understanding." Closing our eyes, and picturing God in the way that the Bible describes is a significant part of setting our mind on things above.

THE POWER OF SETTING OUR MINDS

God has given us a mind with a holy spiritual movie screen called the imagination or our spiritual eyes. On this same screen, God communicates things to us in the form of prophecy, but also His physical beauty in the heavenly realm. We step into and experience spiritual realities as we set our minds on God. Meditation is more than just thinking about God and being inspired. Meditation connects the rest of our being with the spiritual reality that our spirit-man experiences all the time. I truly believe that our thoughts and imagination are God's ordained doorway into the spiritual realm, and if given enough time to be focused on Him, it will transform us.[2]

> *But we all, with unveiled face, beholding as in a mirror the glory of the Lord, are being transformed in the same image from glory to glory, just as by the Spirit of the Lord.*—2 Corinthians 3:18

When you close your eyes to picture God, a faint image will begin to form based on the Biblical descriptions you're meditating on. In 2 Corinthians 3:18, Paul talks about beholding the glory of God with our imaginations. One of his points in this verse is that we can behold God's glory but mostly in faint impressions, as in a reflection of an ancient

---

[1] Romans 8:5, 6:6, 11; Philippians 3:19.

[2] Romans 12:1-2; Ephesians 4:23.

mirror. In Paul's day, mirrors gave a dim and general reflection instead of the clear and detailed reflections we see in our mirrors today.

This same verse highlights another point that what we think about and what we picture in our minds releases spiritual light or darkness into our emotions, desires, and bodies. Our inner life is transformed as it receives God's light in the place where we behold and meditate on Him. In Matthew 6:22, Jesus said, *"If your eye is good then your whole body will be full of light, and if your eye is bad then your whole body is full of darkness."* This verse has many applications, but one is that what we look at with our spiritual eyes imparts spiritual power to our entire being.

I picture our spiritual eyes as being doorways in the spiritual realm that let in whatever they look at whether that be God's light or demonic darkness. When we close our eyes and behold God's faint image, His light and glory supernaturally fill our spiritual eyes and go into the rest of our being to bring light and life. When we behold specific aspects of His presence, that presence illuminates the rest of our being.

In the same vein, our beings can be infected with darkness if we look at darkness with our eyes or behold darkness with our imaginations. In context to Matthew 6, areas of darkness include imagining immorality, money, and anger. When you view or imagine immoral images, imagine wealth, or imagine playing out anger towards others, they stir up all kinds of sinful passions inside. Imagining sinful activities also gives demons legal access to your inner man and body.

SEATED IN THE THRONE ROOM

Or do you not know that as many of us as were baptized into Christ Jesus were baptized into His death? Therefore we were buried with Him through baptism into death, that just as Christ was raised from the dead by the glory of the Father, even so we also should walk in newness of life.—Romans 6:3-4

Even when we were dead in trespasses, made us alive together with Christ (by grace you have been saved), and raised us up together, and made us sit together in the heavenly places in Christ Jesus.—Ephesians 2:5-6

For through Him we both have access by one Spirit to the Father.
—Ephesians 2:18

Our spirits have been given literal access to God's throne room and seated on thrones with Him. We can gaze on God in His throne room and experience Him because our spirit-man has direct access there through our union with Jesus. In a spiritual sense, we have been joined to Him in His death, burial, resurrection, ascension, and enthronement in heaven.[3] In Ephesians 2:5-6, Paul says our spirit-man has been raised up or brought up to heaven with Jesus and made to sit together with Him in the throne room. In fact, we are already citizens of heaven, and our names have already been registered in the city's book.[4] Our bodies will experience the fullness of these realities at Jesus' second coming, but our spirit- man is already experiencing the benefits.

These verses and these spiritual realities have incredible implications on our identities in Christ and our partnership with Him in prayer, but my main point in this section is that we have access to gaze on God's manifest beauty with the eyes of our spirit. This is the good news of the gospel. Jesus has brought us into the beauty realm of God to be stunned and amazed as we look on and behold the uncreated God in all His splendor! He wants to fascinate us and satisfy us as we drink from the holy river of His indescribable glory!

LITERAL TEMPLE AND THRONE ROOM

There is a literal temple in heaven where Jesus and the Father sit enthroned. This is the temple that Jesus has given us access to through His blood. Temple and throne room are synonymous in God's perspective. The Old Testament priests needed the blood of a sacrifice to have access to God's presence in the Holy of holies. Likewise, we needed Jesus' blood to make a way into God's presence. But Jesus' blood was superior to the blood of animals. His blood didn't cleanse a human-made temple on the earth; it cleansed a temple that God made in heaven and reconciled us to God's manifest presence in that place.

Therefore it was necessary that the copies of the things in the heavens should be purified with these, but the heavenly things themselves with better sacrifices

---

[3] Romans 6:3-5.
[4] Hebrews 12:22-23; Philippians 3:20.

than these. For Christ has not entered the holy places made with hands, which are copies of the true, but into heaven itself, now to appear in the presence of God for us.—Hebrews 9:23-24

But Christ came as a High Priest of the good things to come, with the greater and more perfect tabernacle not made with hands, that is, not of this creation. —Hebrews 9:11

Hebrews highlights the reality that the earthly temples were only copies of the temple in heaven from God's perspective.[5] God showed Moses and King David the heavenly temples and instructed them to make divine copies on the earth. This means the earthly temples replicated parts of the heavenly temple, and that there is in fact a literal temple in heaven. Just as the High Priests sprinkled blood and entered God's presence in the earthly temple, Jesus entered into "heaven itself, now to appear in the presence of God for us." Jesus is the High Priest of a temple "not made with hands, that is, not of this creation." The earthly temples were copies of a "greater and more perfect tabernacle."

Therefore brethren, having boldness to enter the holiest by the blood of Jesus, by a new and living way which He consecrated for us, through the veil, that is, His flesh. —Hebrews 10:19-20

Not with the blood of goats and calves, but with His own blood He entered the Most Holy Place once and for all, having obtained eternal redemption. —Hebrews 9:12

Jesus has made a way for us to literally come into the Holy of holies in His heavenly temple to live in the manifest presence of the Father. None of this is symbolic. His blood was real, and the heavenly temple is real. His manifest presence in that temple and our access is real. Jesus ministers as a Priest in this temple, and He beckons us to enter in with Him.

When we close our eyes and set our minds on things above, we access this temple and interact with God. Our spirit-man lives in this temple through our union with Jesus.

---

[5] Hebrews 8:5.

When we set our minds on this room, our thoughts and emotions connect with the heavenly atmosphere that our spirit-man experiences. I believe we can see, feel, and hear the whispers of what heaven is like when we set our minds on the descriptions of the throne room and God's beauty with the Spirit.

THE BEAUTY OF BEAUTIES

God is beautiful in two different ways that are deeply connected: His visible physical presence and His personality. I believe King David beheld God's beauty in both ways all the days of his life.[6] God has revealed both areas to us in the Bible, and they both speak into each other. God's physical presence is detailed and glorious, and it's a direct extension of God's personality because it is part of His being. The exterior glory reveals God's thoughts and emotions, because like other artists, the painting displays the inner workings of the painter.

His inward beauty is connected to His outer beauty and is released and experienced through the outer beauty. The glorious light that radiates from God comes from within Him and carries with it the experiential revelation of His personality. God reveals the hidden things of His heart in the visible glory around Him. The two expressions of beauty are one reality in God.

The throne room is the most beautiful and pleasure-filled place in the entire universe. All of creation reflects God's beauty and flows from His creativity. However, in the throne room, God's raw, uncreated, unveiled beauty dwells in fullness. All of creation is an expression of His artwork and displays Him. But there is a difference when the beauty is God Himself, not an extension or representation or reflection of Him. God has reserved the fullness of creativity and beauty for His dwelling place. It is the climax of heaven and the pinnacle of all beauty, joy, and pleasure. Life, breath, color, fragrance, power, and satisfaction pour out of His being. There is no place like this room, and there is no higher experience than God!

This next idea may sound strange at first, but God loves beauty and pleasure, and He loves to experience them. He invented the idea of beauty in the beginning, and things are only beautiful because He fashioned them. God is the master artist who divinely painted the vast galaxies and sunsets down to the colors and designs of the flowers that capture

---

[6] Psalm 27:4.

our attention. He loves beauty, and it flows out of Him like a mighty river. If God has displayed such beauty in creation, which is tainted by sin right now but still causes us to marvel, how much more His throne room and His actual presence? How much more detailed, and creative, and expressive would God be when creating His very own dwelling place.

Not only does He love beauty, but He also puts a longing for beauty within us. Everybody longs to see beauty and can identify beauty, and everybody experiences a sense of satisfaction when seeing it. This is only true because God has designed us to experience it and be the most satisfied in that experience. God has wired us to long for fascination in Him, and He has given us the capacity to gaze on Him now and in eternity.

This topic is foundational and essential to your prayer life because prayer is meant to be a discovery of the person of God that leads to encounter and fascination. And if God has revealed Himself the most in the throne room, that should be the starting place of discovering God.

WEEKLY ASSIGNMENT

Your assignment this week is to familiarize yourself with the main verses that describe God's throne room (Revelation 4; Exodus 19:18-20; Ezekiel 1:4-28; Isaiah 6:1-4; Daniel 7:9-10). Spend time reading through them, and then briefly read and pray out phrases from Revelation 4 as it's the main chapter the next chapters will build on. As you pray out phrases, try to picture the descriptions, and watch the Holy Spirit make the throne room more real.

29

GOD'S THRONE & GLORIOUS COLORS

INTRODUCTION

These next three chapters will equip you to understand the various passages that describe God's throne room. Each description will have a short explanation, verse references, an example of how I would picture it, and examples of how I would meditate on it. These chapters go verse by verse through Revelation chapter 4 and tie in the other foundational chapters.

There are a lot of descriptions of the throne room, so don't be overwhelmed. This module is only an introduction to the topic. The main purpose of reading through the throne room verses and picturing them in meditation is to begin your journey of seeing God in the Spirit. As you start to incorporate gazing on God in your everyday times with Him, you will probably only focus on one or two descriptions at a time. Over months of doing this, the Holy Spirit will help you begin to see multiple descriptions come together at the same time to see a fuller picture and experience of what's happening around the throne. Your role is to cultivate eyes that see God by setting your mind on one description at a time in meditation. His role is to bring you into an encounter so that what you set your mind on becomes a supernatural impression, and you end up just gazing in awe and wonder.

ENGAGING A PERSON

Focusing on God will lead you to a greater sense of intimacy with Him in prayer. I have experienced this, and I hear this testimony repeatedly from those around me. When you picture God right in front of you, it transforms prayer! When the throne room scene becomes more real, your sense of talking to a real Person will greatly increase. Prayer is so much more enjoyable and tangible when God feels like a living Person who is fully present. It will also produce sobriety and faith that He hears everything you say to Him and that the mighty One on the throne has the power to accomplish His purposes.

When I connect to God visually, everything about my time with Him in that moment completely changes. He's no longer distant and far off in heaven or vague and invisible, which makes my heart disconnect in unbelief. Initially, visualizing Him may take a lot of conscious effort, but taking time to picture God next to you or in the throne room will make your times with Him far more intimate.

IN THE SPIRIT (REVELATION 4:2)

John entered into the spiritual realm, which is where God and all the angels dwell. God is Spirit, and we must enter the spiritual realm to interact with Him.

It is a literal realm that is not seen by the physical eye. John had an open vision, which God may have for you at some point, but even the impression level, seeing in our imagination, is supernatural. We need the Holy Spirit to give us supernatural revelation as we gaze on God to experience it. We position our hearts in meditation and set our minds on the Biblical images and wait for the Spirit to make them alive in our hearts.[1]

BEHOLD (REVELATION 4:2)

The phrase, "I looked and behold," is used about seven different times in Revelation when John is seeing something significant in an open vision.[2] The Greek word for "behold" means to see with our eyes, see with our mind, perceive, become acquainted

---

[1] Ephesians 1:17-19; John 16:13-14, 26; Ezekiel 11:24; 2 Kings 6:17.
[2] Revelation 5:6, 7:9, 14:1, 14:14.

with by experience, and pay attention and respond.[3] John was gripped with fascination in seeing God as he experienced the throne room. His exhortation to us is to behold, pay great attention to this vision, slow down, and gaze upon God until we experience Him and are fascinated like John was.[4]

A THRONE SET IN HEAVEN (REVELATION 4:2)

The first thing John saw in heaven was the Father's throne. It is the center of the universe, and everything receives life and direction from this throne. It is the stability of creation. It is the place where God can rest. God's throne is highlighted about forty times in the book of Revelation because it reveals God's ultimate leadership over the events of creation. John saw all the events of Revelation from the perspective of God being in control on the throne. John Wesley, the famous church leader in the 1700's, said that he was only fearful for a few moments during his life because he saw God ruling all things well on His throne.

God's throne speaks of His power, ownership, authority, involvement, and ultimate responsibility for creation. It also speaks of His wisdom, His ability to see all things and evaluate all things. It also speaks of His divine activity. The Father has all dominion over creation. Everything is His, and He has the right and power to bring to pass the things of His heart. God is King, and He governs from the throne. Every plan and decision is made and then decreed from the throne.

God's throne is set and established in heaven. It is immovable and unshakeable. It has been established and planted from eternity and nothing can overcome His power, *"The LORD has established His throne in the heavens, and His kingdom rules over all."*[5] He is enthroned with power and rules righteously over all of creation, *"But the LORD sits enthroned forever; He has established His throne for justice, and He judges the world with righteousness; He judges the people with uprightness."*[6]

---

3 Strong's Greek #3708 - https://www.studylight.org/lexicons/greek/3708.html
4 Psalm 27:4; Revelation 5:6, 7:9, 14:14, 19:11.
5 Psalm 103:19.
6 Psalm 9:7.

FATHER'S THRONE

I watched till thrones were put in place, and the Ancient of Days was seated;
His garment was white as snow, and the hair of His head was like pure wool.
His throne was a fiery flame, its wheels a burning fire; a fiery stream issued
and came forth from before Him.—Daniel 7:9-10

The Father's throne is a fiery flame. His throne is a raging fire with chariot- like wheels that are also on fire. The fire could speak of His all-consuming power, which burns up everything that hinders His kingdom and His absolute purity in all the things that He does. Revelation 20 describes the Father's throne as the great white throne on which He judges the dead. His throne is great in size, strength, and majesty, and it is a magnificent white color that radiates purity and light.

Out of the Father's throne comes forth a river of fire, which I believe is the river of life that comes out of God's throne, *"And he showed me a pure river of water of life, clear as crystal, proceeding from the throne of God and of the Lamb."*[7] This river flows from God as its source, and it brings God's life wherever it goes.

JESUS' THRONE

And above the firmament over their heads was the likeness of a throne, in
appearance like a sapphire stone.—Ezekiel 1:27

Jesus' throne is next to the Father's throne.[8] Ezekiel saw Jesus' throne as a deep blue sapphire color, which is the same color and make-up as the sea of glass that makes up the floor in the throne room.[9] It's common to believe that the sapphire mentioned in the Bible is now called lapis lazuli. It has a true-blue color to it with reflective gold-like particles inside it.[10] I'm assuming it has a blue color to it like the sky, but with a supernatural

---

7 Revelation 22:1.
8 Revelation 22:1; Hebrews 8:1; Psalm 110:1.
9 Exodus 24:10.
10 Hobart King, "Lapis Lazuli," Geology.com.
    https://geology.com/gemstones/lapis-lazuli/

clearness to it like crystal. His throne may be the same color as the sea of glass because it speaks of His involvement and connection to creation as a Man and His supremacy over creation as the King on the throne above the heavens.[11]

EXAMPLE IMAGES

I picture myself in front of Jesus' throne and the Father's throne, and I slowly picture their thrones' colors and qualities. Their thrones are majestic and stately and full of authority. I picture the Father on His fiery throne, and I see a vast bright bonfire. I visualize it, and then I listen to the sounds of the flames moving and burning. Next to the Father, I picture Jesus' throne with the deep but clear sapphire color with movement and supernatural clarity. I feel the weight and power of the Father's and Jesus' leadership over creation. They are the Creator and have all the rights to lead and the power to lead.

Then I picture the river of life surging out of their thrones. I picture myself standing in the middle of it to receive the life and fire of God. These thrones are the center of the universe and the source of all life.

EXAMPLE MEDITATION

Abba, You are sitting on Your throne. You are the center of the universe and the sustainer of all things. You have made all things, and You govern all things. This is the place where You rest and rule all things. You are the Creator, and all things are under Your control. Your throne will never be moved. It has been set and established in heaven above every other throne and power in the heavens and on the earth. The foundation of Your throne is justice and righteousness. Every decision You make is perfect in justice, and every command You make is righteous in its execution. You see all things, and I trust You to lead my life and to lead creation into the fullness of Your plans. Your throne is a fiery flame. You are the all-consuming fire sitting on the throne of fire. You designed Your throne, and it is majestic. There is no throne like Yours. You burn up everything that resists You and Your kingdom. You are filled with desire and zeal to fill the earth with Your glory, and nothing will stop You. I gaze at You on Your fiery throne, Father. Jesus, Your

---

Joseph Jacobs and Immanuel Benzinger, "Sapphire," Jewish Encyclopedia online http://www.jewishencyclopedia.com/articles/13190-sapphire

[11] Other verse references for God's throne - Psalm 9:4-7, 11:4, 47:8, 89:14, 93:2, 97:2, 103:19; Job 26:9; Isaiah 6:1-4; 66:1; 1 Kings 22:19, 22.

throne is the deep blue sapphire of the sky. Jesus, You are sitting on Your sapphire throne. You are the only Man that sits on God's throne. Your throne is beautiful as it flows into the sea of glass around You.

JASPER AND SARDIUS STONE (REVELATION 4:3)

Many people believe the jasper stone was a clear diamond-like color, while the sardius stone was a deep, red-colored stone. John saw the Father shining like a bright white and burning red diamond. The glory that comes from God's being has color to it.

JASPER - CLEAR DIAMOND

The jasper stone is mentioned three other times in Revelation to describe the wall around the New Jerusalem and the glorious light that comes from it, *"The great city, the holy Jerusalem, descending out of heaven from God, having the glory of God. Her light was like the most precious stone, like a jasper stone, clear as crystal."*[12]

> *Who cover Yourself with light as with a garment, who stretch out the heavens like a curtain.*—Psalm 104:2

> *Who alone has immortality, dwelling in unapproachable light, whom no man has seen or can see.*—1 Timothy 6:16

There is a layer of bright light that comes from the Father and surrounds Him. Psalm 104 says that God has wrapped Himself with a garment of light. Uncreated light and splendor surround Him. His light is so glorious and so unique that it even outshines the brightest sun and overwhelms those around Him.[13] This brilliant white light could speak of His absolute purity and beauty.

---

[12] Revelation 21:10-11.
[13] Revelation 1:16, 21:23; Matthew 17:2; Isaiah 24:23, 60:19.

SARDIUS - RED

The sardius stone color could speak of His burning desire. God is literally an all-consuming fire that is passionate and jealous for all of our love.[14] He burns on the inside of Himself for the ones that He loves, and His fiery love cannot be extinguished. The One on the throne is passionate and involved in the story of creation and He will bring His plans to completion. He is not disconnected from creation; instead, He is 100% emotionally involved and invested in bringing things to fullness.

God's fire and bright light are combined in other Biblical encounters. Ezekiel saw the combination of God's glory like bright light and burning fire, *"Also from the appearance of His waist and upward I saw as it were, the color of amber with the appearance of fire all around within it; and from the waist and downward I saw, as it were, the appearance of fire with brightness all around."*[15] Daniel also saw the glory of God like brightness and fire, *"And the Ancient of Days was seated; His garment was white as snow, and the hair of His head was like pure wool, His throne was a fiery flame, its wheels a burning fire; a fiery stream issued and came forth from before Him."*[16]

INTERNAL AND EXTERNAL BEAUTY

God's colorful light reveals Him in two different ways: it represents aspects of His heart, and it's a literal and visible expression of His heart. I believe His light has substance to it that releases an intimate experience with aspects of God's heart to those around Him. His light's substance is a tangible presence that can be felt, a fragrance that can be smelled, and revelation that can be experienced. The light of God's glory is the knowledge of God, which means that His light is the physical expression of His personality.[17] Waves of light pass over the millions of saints and angels and cause them to experience God and bow down in worship.

I think there are colors coming from God that have never been seen on the earth before, all of which express different aspects of His personality and release encounter with God. There may be one color that visibly express His humility, another His love, another His peace, another His joy, another His burning desire, and so on. From a scientific

[14] Hebrews 12:29; Deuteronomy 4:24.
[15] Ezekiel 1:27.
[16] Daniel 7:9.
[17] 2 Corinthians 4:6.

perspective, God has made our eyes to only see light. Light and colors are made up of energy waves, with every color having its own frequency. When light comes into our eyes, the energy's frequency gets processed, and then information is passed onto our minds as colors. Our eyes only perceive light, which I believe is another statement of how we were physically and spiritually made to gaze on God's beauty and experience Him.[18]

EXAMPLE IMAGES

First, I picture God as a giant bonfire with flames moving all around Him. Then I imagine progressive waves of glorious bright light coming off God to reveal Himself to those in the temple. The light would be blinding in the natural like the sun is on a clear day, but God's light is different. I picture those waves coming off Him and sweeping across the millions of angels and humans in the temple. As the light comes to them, they experience God supernaturally. I picture various colors flowing together in His glory, and I imagine the colors being alive with His life.

EXAMPLE MEDITATION

You are shining and filling heaven with all Your beauty. Light and life and burning desire break out from Your being and fill my heart with wonder. Your light is filled with life and revelation. Uncreated light. Uncreated beauty. My eyes were made to see You, God. Waves of Your marvelous light pass over again and again as I stand before You. Your colorful light is filled with the substance, and it releases encounters with Your heart. Your burning fire is Your burning passion for deep friendship with me. You love me with all Your heart, soul, mind, and strength, and You are jealous for all of me. You burn with a deep fiery passion. Uncontainable desire surges through Your being and comes out as fire.

A RAINBOW AROUND THE THRONE (REVELATION 4:3)

There is an emerald-green rainbow covering God's throne. The Greek word used for the rainbow in this verse gives the idea that the rainbow is more like a dome or halo than just a single strip of a rainbow.[19] John and Ezekiel both saw something like a rainbow over the throne of God, *"Like the appearance of a rainbow*

---

[18] Other verse references for God's light - Psalm 36:9; John 1:5; Colossians 1:12; 1 John 1:5.

[19] Strong's Greek #2943 - https://www.studylight.org/lexicons/eng/greek/2943.html

in a cloud on a rainy day, so was the appearance of the brightness all around it. This was the appearance of the likeness of the glory of the LORD.[20]

> *And God said: "This is the sign of the covenant which I make between Me and you, and every living creature that is with you, for perpetual generations: I set My rainbow in the cloud, and it shall be for the sign of the covenant between Me and the earth. It shall be when I bring a cloud over the earth, that the rainbow shall be seen in the cloud; and I will remember My covenant which is between Me and you and every living creature of all flesh; the waters shall never again become a flood to destroy all flesh.—Genesis 9:12-15*

The rainbow imagery is from the days of Noah, and it expresses God's sovereignty and His tender mercy. The rainbow is an everlasting sign of God's covenant with Noah and creation that He would be faithful to bring His covenant people through trouble. God sends a rainbow to the earth every time it rains to remind us that He will keep His promises. God looks at the earthly rainbows and thinks about His covenant with Noah. John saw the throne and the rainbow around God just before seeing the end-time flood of judgments, which implies God's mercy will still be evident amid wrath.

The rainbow speaks of God's desire to show mercy. The mercy rainbow covers the throne because everything God thinks and does is under the banner of mercy. In the Old Testament time frame, God's throne was in the Holy of holies in the temple as represented by the top of the ark of the covenant called the mercy seat. The blood of the sacrifice was sprinkled on the mercy seat to reconcile God and man.[21] The mercy seat was God's throne in the temple, which is powerful because His throne was called the place of mercy. Psalm 145:8-9 says that all that God does is under the banner of mercy. Even His judgments are filled with mercy because they are meant to awaken a love response and are progressively and methodically released.

EXAMPLE IMAGES

When I pray, I picture a beautiful, majestic, and huge dome-shaped rainbow standing clearly above God's glory on the throne. It has more colors than we know of on the earth.

---

[20] Ezekiel 1:28.
[21] Leviticus 16:14.

I picture all those on the sea of glass as being able to see this great and colorful structure surrounding God's glory. I thank Him for His mercy and for His eternal promise to honor the covenant with Noah and creation. I thank Him for His commitment to bringing creation into the fullness of what He has always planned.

EXAMPLE MEDITATION

There is a radiant rainbow around Your glory and Your throne. There is a shining emerald rainbow around You. Your rainbow is beautiful, Abba, all-encompassing and surrounding Your light with even more color. Your rainbow is extravagant in beauty and colors that amaze me. The colors are moving. The colors are vast and different than anything I've ever seen. I love to gaze on Your rainbow and remember Your mercy. You are slow to anger and great in mercy, and Your tender mercies cover all Your works. You remember Your commitments to Noah and creation, and the decisions You make on the throne are for mercy. Your throne decisions are under the banner of the mercy rainbow. Everything You think and do is within the covenants You have made and Your desire for mercy.

WEEKLY ASSIGNMENT

Your assignment this week is to take at least one prayer time to practice picturing the Biblical descriptions of God, His throne, and the rainbow around the throne. During your time, write down what you saw with your spiritual eyes, what you felt, and what you talked about with God. To get a rhythm in these descriptions, I encourage you to picture them during all your prayer and worship times this week. If you want to do an extra bonus, do a simple word study on the word "throne." Type the word in a Bible search website and read through every verse that references God's throne. Write down any information that is helpful to you.

DISCIPLESHIP MEETING GUIDE
MODULE 7: THRONE ROOM – CHAPTERS 28 & 29

MEETING FOCUS:

The purpose of this week's meeting is to discuss the spiritual principle of setting our minds on God's image in the throne room and to process the meditation assignment.

DISCUSSION QUESTIONS (IN ORDER OF IMPORTANCE):

1. ***Spiritual Pursuits:***
   a. Practically, how is your prayer schedule going? How many days have you walked out your prayer schedule? Do you need to make small changes to your schedule? How are your daily prayer times going, and how is God impacting you through them?
   b. Briefly review your new *Spiritual Pursuits Document*.

2. ***Chapter Questions:***
   a. Chapter 28 – Discuss any of your journaled thoughts and questions. What are your thoughts and questions on setting your mind on the throne room and having access to God's throne room by Jesus' blood?
   b. Chapter 29 – In-depth, share how your throne room meditation time went.

3. ***Heart Issue:***
   a. Share how your heart issue has been going this past week. With heart issue discussions, process, confess, encourage, and pray together for God to release transformation. ***Pray in tongues together and ask God to release power to the heart issue.***

4. Briefly review the assignments for the next two weeks together.

MEETING NOTES:

_____

_____

_____

_____

_____

_____

_____

_____

_____

_____

_____

_____

30

GOD'S GLORY STORM

MY TESTIMONY

Gazing on God in the throne room has significantly impacted my relationship with God. For the first couple of years of pursuing God in prayer, I was hindered by a distracted mind, and I was disconnected from experiencing God as a present-tense person in my interactions with Him.

At some point, I began to engage my imagination by picturing myself praying in a valley near God's Mountain, and it made my experience more real. I used that image until I heard a teaching on God's throne room. I took a few months to study the Biblical descriptions and began to get a growing picture in my imagination of God's throne room. Little by little, I began to experience the living reality of the throne room in my times with God, and it changed my prayer life. The scene became real, and it became quick and easy to step into the scene whenever I engaged with God in any way.

In one specific season, a friend and I would pray around the truths of Revelation 4 a couple days a week for an hour. We would pray and sing in the spirit and then take turns speaking out the realities of the verses one phrase at a time, similar to a group meditation time. As we did that, we would experience the things we were focused on. The images would become a little more tangible. The sounds or colors or ideas would become alive to us, and sometimes it felt like the presence of that idea was manifested in our room, even if just a little. Sometimes God would touch our hearts in a clear way, and we would be filled with tears, joy, awe, and worship. I've never had an open vision of heaven, but at the impression level, I can always see, hear, and feel things in God's throne room that I believe to be real in heaven. At times, I sense the faint sounds of the raging fire of the Father's throne or the choruses of the living creatures as they sing of God's beauty. Sometimes I feel the trembling power of the lightning and thunder around God or feel the glory of walking on the crystal sea mingled with fire as I pace in prayer.

I share all of this because I want you to know you can have a consistent supernatural (faint impressions) experience with God in context to His throne room. This consistent experience doesn't happen overnight, but if you see the truth of the scriptures and respond with time and meditation *until* you begin to experience it, you will be changed! This reality is for every believer, not just for elite prayer people, spiritually gifted seers, or certain personalities. It's for those that are hungry enough to say yes to the prayer process until they experience something more substantial.

Challenge the lie that an experience isn't available to you because it doesn't happen right away or because of the initial difficulties. God has brought you into the Holy of holies in heaven because He desires face-to-face communion with you. God has designed you with spiritual eyes and spiritual senses to engage with Him, and He will be faithful to shine His light on you as you draw near to Him.

GOD'S GLORY STORM (REVELATION 4:5)

This section includes the cloud of God's presence, lightning and thundering, and the voices that come from God. Around God's Being is the most awesome and terrifying storm. There is a swirling dark cloud that is a raging fire. Out of the cloud of fire, there are lightning, thunder, and voices. I believe all the components of God's storm speak of His power, divine activity, and intervention in the natural realm.

THE CLOUD OF GOD'S PRESENCE

THICK AND DARK CLOUD

Behold, I will come to you in the thick cloud.—Exodus 19:9

So the people stood afar off, but Moses drew near the thick darkness where God was.—Exodus 20:21

The LORD reigns; let the earth rejoice; let the multitude of isles be glad! Clouds and darkness surround Him; righteousness and justice are the foundation of His throne.—Psalm 97:1-2

God surrounds Himself with a thick and dark cloud of glory that is an extension of His being. To touch the cloud is to touch God and experience Him. It's moving and alive and releases an experience with God's heart in the midst of it. The cloud has enough divine substance and texture to it that God calls it thick. Earthly clouds are made of water droplets and dust, but God's cloud is tangible and is composed of His weighty substance so that people even fall in His presence. The cloud is dark in color, but it seems that even the darkness has substance because Moses called it thick darkness.

God consistently manifested Himself to Israel inside of His glory cloud through the books of Exodus, Leviticus, Numbers, and Deuteronomy. During the exodus from Egypt, God walked in front of Israel inside of a cloudy pillar during the day. Moses saw a thick and dark cloud cover Mt. Sinai. When God would meet with Moses in the tabernacle of meeting, He would descend through a cloudy pillar. The dark glory cloud filled Solomon's temple, The Father appeared to Jesus in a cloud on the Mount of Transfiguration, and Jesus said He would come back on the clouds of heaven with power and glory.[1]

FIERY CLOUD

Now Mount Sinai was completely in smoke, because the LORD descended upon it in fire. Its smoke ascended like the smoke of a furnace and the whole mountain quaked greatly.—Exodus 19:18

Then I looked, and behold, a whirlwind was coming out of the north, a great cloud with raging fire engulfing itself.—Ezekiel 1:4

---

[1] Matthew 24:30.

The glory cloud has a supernatural dimension of fire that burns within it. God is an all-consuming fire of love, desire, and power, and a fire extends from His being within the cloud. The cloud that descended on Mt. Sinai was burning with an all-consuming fire that caused the mountain to smoke. Ezekiel saw the glory cloud of God like a whirlwind and saw a raging fire within the cloud.

RADIATING LIGHT

Then I looked, and behold, a whirlwind was coming out of the north, a great cloud with raging fire engulfing itself; and brightness was all around it and radiating out of its midst like the color of amber, out of the midst of the fire.—Ezekiel 1:4

While He was still speaking, behold, a bright cloud overshadowed them; and suddenly a voice came out of the cloud, saying, "This is My beloved Son, in whom I am well pleased. Hear Him!—Matthew 19:7

The fiery cloud has a glorious light or brightness that is within and shines out of it. Ezekiel saw the raging fire with amber light radiating out of the midst of it. On the Mount of Transfiguration, the Father manifested to Jesus and the others in a cloud that had a brightness to it.

In summary, the cloud has several components. It's a dark cloud that also has brightness shining out of it. It is a cloud by itself, but there is a supernatural fire with smoke rising from the fire inside the cloud. The cloud has physical and spiritual substance because it's called God's glory, and at times people are unable to stand when the glory cloud is manifest.

EXAMPLE IMAGES

I picture a massive storm cloud that is on fire and swirling around God on His throne. I imagine a raging fire within the cloud, and I listen to the sounds of the flames burning. I picture the smoke of the fire rising higher and higher. Then I imagine a brilliant light coming out of the cloud. I often have a sense of the majesty of God with this imagery. I stand outside the cloud to gaze on it, and then I enter into it to stand and experience His glory. I picture the brightness pervading the substance of the cloud, almost like bright sparkles within the darkness. I take time to feel the substance of the cloud as it is the extension of God Himself.

EXAMPLE MEDITATION

You dwell in a thick and dark cloud. You have a cloud that is made of supernatural substance. Your uncreated and raw power is within the mysterious cloud. Your cloud is Your glory. You cover the face of Your throne with Your cloud, and You make darkness Your hiding place. Who are You, God? Why do You dwell within the cloud? What is the cloud made from? What kind of substance is the cloud? It is Your glory. You are awesome in power, and I tremble before You. That swirling cloud of fire is all around You. That glorious and dark cloud is all around You. It is glorious with its heavenly light shining out. It is amazing with the light of Your face shining out. Oh, the majestic storm of God. The sight of Your glory is like a consuming fire within the cloud. You are a pillar of cloud and a pillar of fire with God as the source.

OTHER VERSE REFERENCES

Exodus 13:21, 14:24, 16:10, 24:16, 34:5, 40:35; Leviticus 16:2; Numbers 12:5; Deuteronomy 4:11, 33:26; 2 Samuel 22:12; 1 Kings 8:11; 2 Chronicles 5:13; Job 22:14, 26:9; Psalm 18:11, 68:4, 32-34, 104:3; Isaiah 4:5; 19:1; Ezekiel 10:4; Daniel 7:13; Nahum 1:3; Matthew 24:30, 26:64; Acts 1:9; 1 Thessalonians 4:17; Revelation 1:7, 14:14.

LIGHTNING AND THUNDERING

Then it came to pass on the third day, in the morning, that there were thunderings and lightnings, and a thick cloud on the mountain.—Exodus 19:16

At Your rebuke they fled; at the voice of Your thunder they hastened away.—Psalm 104:7

He sent out arrows and scattered them; lightning bolts, and He vanquished them.—2 Samuel 22:15

Lightning and thundering are within God's glory cloud. Throughout the book of Revelation in heaven, they are seen just before God moves in power to confront the darkness in the earthly realm.[2] Throughout Revelation and in many other passages, His lightning and thundering represent His divine activity and divine intervention in bringing justice. It's like He flexes His mighty arm by releasing raw power around the throne in the expression of lightning and thundering. I believe they release power encounters to those in the throne room as flashes of power break out from His being.

In the earthly realm, a lightning bolt is created by an incredible electrical charge in a storm cloud that can increase the air temperature by 50,000 degrees Fahrenheit, which is about five times hotter than the surface of the Sun. Thunder is the result of the air's heating and cooling around the lightning, which then creates sound waves that can be heard up to fifteen miles away.[3] In the heavenly realm, God is the source of the power that creates lightning and thunder. What kind of power is surging from Him in the throne room atmosphere if the earthly demonstration is so powerful?[4]

EXAMPLE IMAGES

I picture His lightning releasing overwhelming flashes of light all around the throne room, and I listen to His thunder shaking the atmosphere. Flashes of supernatural lightning break out from His being at different moments and fill the throne room with incredible ongoing streaks of light. I picture those streaks going over the masses of angels and saints on the sea of glass around the throne and striking them with raw power encounters with God. His thunder communicates who He is with a sound that has life and substance to it. His thunder overwhelms the senses in the best way. His glory storm is something to be absorbed in and lost in with the experience of awe, wonder, and fascination— and in humility when we know He is God, and we are but dust. His power isn't to be figured out and primarily analyzed, but first to be experienced and then be undone by, as we stand in awe before the infinite God Who is beyond our comprehension.

Picture yourself within the loudest and most powerful storm you've ever seen, and then multiply it by 100 to get a starting point for God's storm. I remember one storm years

---

[2] Revelation 4:5, 8:5, 11:19, 16:18.

[3] "Understanding Lightning Science." https://www.weather.gov/safety/lightning-science-overview

[4] Other verse references for God's lightning and thunder - Exodus 9:23; 1 Samuel 2:10, 7:10; Psalm 18:13-14, 29:3, 77:18, 81:7, 97:4; Job 26:14, 36:32; Habakkuk 3:4; Zechariah 9:14.

ago that was rumbling from miles away and filling the sky with ominous darkness. At the same time, unending massive streaks of lighting were breaking out and weaving in every direction in a way that lit up the sky. My friends and I were captivated by the power of the storm, so we went outside to experience it. As we stood outside, a bolt of lightning seemed to hit the ground in our area. The ground shook, and an incredible sound of thunder filled the atmosphere and shook us to the core. We all fell to the ground in fear and ran inside trembling. It was awesome! I imagine the atmosphere around God to be filled with this same vibrancy and electric life.

EXAMPLE MEDITATION

You are mighty within the storm. You are glorious and majestic and powerful. All power is Yours. The shaking power of lightning and thunder flows out of Your being. There is no external source, just the raw power of Your being. Flashes of lightning breaking out from the center of the universe, the throne of God. They   break out and branch out in the upper atmosphere of the heavenly throne room. They flash from Your being and strike the masses of people on the sea of glass with the raw power of God. Saints and angels are falling under the power of God that is breaking out from the throne. I love the lightning of Your presence. I love the thunder of Your presence. You shake me to the core with the power and energy in Your thunder. I'm in awe of You, God. You are infinite and uncreated, and I am finite and created. You fascinate me with the levels of power that come from You, that same infinite power that created and now sustains every molecule of the universe. Who can understand the power of Your thunder? Who can understand the power that surges from You in the voice of Your thunder? You are mighty in heaven, and Your storm is the visible manifestation of the zeal that it is in Your heart to bring justice to the earth.

VOICES FROM THE THRONE

The Lord thundered from heaven, and the Most High uttered His voice. —2 Samuel 22:14

Hear attentively the thunder of His voice, and the rumbling that comes from His mouth….After it a voice roars; He thunders with His majestic voice, And

He does not restrain them when His voice is heard. God thunders marvelously with His voice; He does great things which we cannot comprehend.—Job 37:2

Now My soul is troubled, and what shall I say? "Father, save Me from this hour?" But for this purpose I came to this hour. Father, glorify Your name." Then a voice came from heaven, saying, "I have both glorified it and will glorify it again." Therefore the people who stood by and heard it said that it had thundered. Others said, "An angel has spoken to Him."—John 12:27-29

There are also voices coming out of the midst of the storm and proceeding from the throne of God. The voices must be God's voice because they're coming from His throne. In other Revelation passages, a voice comes from the midst of the four living creatures, the altar, the heavenly temple, or from heaven, which seem more general as to who is actually speaking. The Greek word for voices means a literal voice or a sound from an instrument or other inanimate objects.[5] This word is used about fifty times in Revelation alone. Most of the time, it refers to God's voice or an angel's voice, but several times it refers to the sound of an instrument or something moving. Some Bibles translate it as "rumblings" or "sounds" instead of "voices" to connect it to the sound of thunder.

I believe the voices are God's voice speaking, singing, and even the sound of music coming from Jesus, the Father, and the Spirit. His voice could sound like a trumpet, the flowing of many waters, and even sound like thunder.[6] I think it's also possible that the thunder that comes from His throne is an actual sound, but that it also carries with it the voice of God. In Revelation 10, seven thunders are personified and have voices that prophesy concerning the future. The seven thunders have voices and can articulate words, but they still have the sound of thunder.[7]

God's manifestation on Mount Sinai references trumpets blasting but doesn't explicitly say people heard God's voice, but Hebrews quotes the story and says it was God's voice that shook the earth.[8] It's possible that His voice was in the trumpet blast or that Exodus 19 just doesn't list His voice as shaking the earth. Because of the seven

---

[5] Strong's Greek #5456 - https://www.studylight.org/lexicons/greek/5456.html

[6] Revelation 1:10, 15, 4:1, 14:2.

[7] Other verse references for God's thunderous voice - Job 40:9; Psalm 18:13, 29:3, 77:18; Ezekiel 3:12.

[8] Hebrews 12:18-19, 26.

thunders having voices and because the trumpet on Mount Sinai possibly being connected to God's voice, I think it's possible that the thunder and His voice are connected in a way that seems impossible to us in the natural realm. It is significant to note that in the Bible God's voice is mostly compared to thunder.

EXAMPLE IMAGES

I picture myself standing before the glory storm of God, listening for various ways in which He might speak. I ask Him to talk to me about the things that are on His heart so that I can know Him as a friend and so that I can partner with Him as a witness on the earth. Sometimes, at the impression level, I hear His voice like thunder in my heart, and sometimes I hear Him singing things to me and over me.

EXAMPLE MEDITATION

Here I am, Abba. Speak to me, sing to me, thunder over me. I open my heart to hear the majesty of Your voice. You are a real person with real thoughts and emotions that You want to communicate to me in words. You have a voice. God has a voice. Songs and melodies are flowing out of Your being. Voices are proceeding from the throne that those in heaven can hear—real voices from the Almighty. You are musical and filled with songs and declarations for Your people.

WEEKLY ASSIGNMENT

Your assignment this week is to take at least one prayer time to practice picturing the Biblical descriptions of God's glory storm. During your time, write down what you saw with your spiritual eyes, what you felt, and what you talked about with God. To get a rhythm in these descriptions, I encourage you to picture the throne room descriptions during all your prayer and worship times this week. If you want to do an extra assignment, do a simple word study on clouds, lighting, or thunder. Type these words in a Bible search website and read through every verse that references God's throne room or God's presence. Write down any information that is helpful to you.

31

AROUND GOD'S THRONE

HOLY FASCINATION

One thing I have desired of the Lord, that will I seek; that I may dwell in the house of the Lord all the days of my life, to behold the beauty of the LORD.—Psalm 27:4

God wants to give His people a vision for encounter and fascination in Him that will awaken a wholehearted pursuit. King David had a vision to experience God's beauty, and that vision ruined him for anything less. Even as a king with many responsibilities and options for pleasure and entertainment, David had one primary life pursuit; to see God's beauty and experience fascination. David understood that God made him to experience His beauty and to overflow out of that place of encounter into the other areas of his life. David's chief longing through the day was to see God. Even in the midst of challenge and disappointment, which Psalm 27 is about, David was anchored by this one thing. He knew what God made him for, and no circumstance or season could shake him and distract him from the place of encounter.

God has given you eyes to see, ears to hear, and a heart to perceive Him. God wants to fascinate you and satisfy the eternal longings for pleasure and beauty He has put within you as you gaze on Him. He is the joyful and overflowing Bridegroom God who loves to reveal Himself to your heart extravagantly. Stay in the bonfire of His presence, and He will show you more of Himself and begin to ruin you for any lesser pleasure that the earth, the world, or the devil can offer. Let Him wash away your dullness, distractions, and brokenness with the beauty of His holiness.

SEVEN LAMPS (REVELATION 4:5)

And you shall command the children of Israel that they bring you pure oil of pressed olives for the light, to cause the lamp to burn continually.—Exodus 27:20

Aaron will be in charge of it from evening until morning before the LORD continually; it shall be a statute forever in your generations. He shall be in charge of the lamps on the pure gold lampstand before the LORD continually. —Leviticus 24:3-4

Interestingly, the Holy Spirit manifests Himself as a burning lampstand before God instead of manifesting Himself as a person on a throne like the Father and Son. He is as much God as the Father and the Son. However, there is a reason in God's heart for the Spirit to manifest in this throne room scene as a lampstand.

The lamp image is a direct reference to the Jewish temples where one lampstand was put in the Holy Place right outside of the veil that led into the Holy of Holies. The lampstand was one large golden piece with six individual branches coming off the main branch, making a total of seven branches. At the end of each branch was a flame that was sustained with a wick and oil that was supposed to burn continually and be maintained by the priesthood. The Jewish temples were copies of the heavenly temple, so it is fair to assume this earthly lampstand was modeled after the Holy Spirit's lampstand in Revelation 4:5.

The lampstand in the earthly temples filled the dark holy place with continual light and represented God's presence, revelation, and truth to His people. It also represented His light and presence upon His covenant people to display His salvation to the nations. I believe these are the same foundational ideas of the heavenly lampstand of the Spirit. He is God's light, presence, and power, revealing the deep things of God to the human heart. The Father and Son are shining from the throne, but the Spirit is also burning and shining the light of the knowledge of God upon His people. He is active in ministering light and truth to God's people around the throne and on the earth.

And I looked, and behold, in the midst of the throne and of the four living creatures, and in the midst of the elders, stood a Lamb as though it had been slain, having seven horns and seven eyes, which are the seven Spirits of God sent out into all the earth.—Revelation 5:6

The lampstand of the Spirit is also the fullness of God's anointing resting upon Jesus as King of Kings. He anoints Jesus to bring salvation and healing to the nations as the Messiah. He is called the seven Spirits of God in relation to the lampstand because seven represents the fullness of His activity and power.[1] He is one Spirit with seven manifestations or expressions. Isaiah prophesied about this seven-fold anointing that would rest upon the Messiah.[2]

EXAMPLE IMAGES

I picture one large lamp, comparable to a tree trunk, with seven branches on it with a fire burning at each branch's end. The details of the lamp are not described, but I picture it as a beautiful clear gold fixture with fire moving through it to the end of the branches. Then I imagine large, powerful flames coming out of all seven branches that touch the bodies and hearts of those around the throne to impart power and the revelation of God. I ask the Spirit to reveal God to me and to be my divine escort into the beauty realm of God. Then I ask for His seven-fold anointing to rest upon me to bring His light and glory to those around me.

EXAMPLE MEDITATION

Seven lamps are burning in Your presence with a holy flame. The Spirit of God is burning in Your presence as lamps that never go out. You are the burning lampstand around the throne. You shine, and You burn, Holy Spirit. You are a servant who brings me into the revelation of the Father and the Son, thank you! Your lampstand shines with great glory and beauty. You are the seven-fold Spirit of God. Your ministry to me is complete. Seven Spirits of God. Seven-fold Spirit of God before the throne. I have the fullness of the Spirit available to me around the throne to bring me into the beauty of God's heart.

---

[1] Revelation 1:4, 3:1, 5:6.
[2] Isaiah 11:1-2.

SEA OF GLASS (REVELATION 4:6)

And they saw the God of Israel. And there was under His feet as it were a paved work of sapphire stone, and it was like the very heavens in its clarity.—Exodus 24:10

The likeness of the firmament above the heads of the living creatures was like the color of an awesome crystal stretched out over their heads.—Ezekiel 1:22

And I saw something like a sea of glass mingled with fire and those who have the victory over the beast, over his image and over his mark and over the number of his name standing on the sea of glass having harps of God.—Revelation 15:2

The floor of the throne room consists of a beautiful transparent crystal. It's a vast floor for a vast throne room, and it goes as far as the eye can see. This floor is what the saints and angels gather on to worship God in heaven. In Revelation 15, John saw the sea of glass a second time, except this time, he saw fire moving inside the crystal. Moses and the elders saw God's throne and a sea of glass underneath it with a sapphire color. Ezekiel saw the sea of glass as an awesome crystal and called it a firmament or an expanse, which is the same language used for a specific layer of the sky in the creation account.

The sea of glass is part of the beauty of the throne room, and it is one of the ways God releases His glory to the people around Him. I believe the fire of God's being moves through the glass and touches the worshipers on it. As light radiates out of God's being, the crystal-like floor with sapphire (blue) color reflects the glorious light of God in every direction like a multifaceted diamond.

It is called the sea of glass because it is boundless like the sea so that you can't see the end of it in any direction. It is transparent like crystal yet has a sapphire blue color to it, which is the same as Jesus' throne in Ezekiel's vision. This connection to Jesus' throne makes it seem like the crystal is a direct extension of His throne.

Praise God in His sanctuary; praise Him in His mighty firmament.
—Psalm 150:1

The sea of glass could also represent God's position over all of creation and His deep involvement in the created order. In this representation, the sea of glass resembles the sky, or the firmament, that divides the heavens. God's throne is on top of the glass, speaking of His throne being over the circle of the earth.[3]

EXAMPLE IMAGES

I begin by picturing an endless crystal floor that goes in every direction. The crystal reflects and carries the glorious light of God to all those in the throne room. I imagine the light of God reflecting at different angles like light passing through a diamond. Then I picture fire from God's throne running through the glass and imparting God's life to His worshipers. When I'm sitting or walking in prayer, I visualize myself moving on the glass as if it's the floor I'm physically standing on in the moment.

EXAMPLE MEDITATION

Here I am, Abba, standing on the sea of glass mingled with the fire that comes from Your throne. I take my place on the glassy pavement and worship You with the host of heaven. Your glory radiates and reflects off the beautiful glass in every direction. There is a river of fire flowing inside the glass that imparts Your fire to my heart. I feel the fire and the substance of the floor as I walk and bow down before You! The crystal floor is alive with Your power and presence. Awesome crystal in every direction. Like the ocean in its length, width, and depth. There is no end in sight to this awesome pavement. It flows out of Your throne, God. It flows out of Your throne like an endless ocean.

ANGELS AND LIVING CREATURES (REVELATION 4:6)

But you have come to Mount Zion and to the city of the living God, the heavenly Jerusalem, to an innumerable company of angels. —Hebrews 12:22

Then I looked and I heard the voice of many angels around the throne, the living creatures, and the elders: The number of them was ten thousand times

---

[3] Genesis 1:8, 14-15.

ten thousand and thousands of thousands saying with a loud voice, "Worthy is the lamb who was slain."—Revelation 5:11-12

There are countless angels of all rank, size, and glory around God. They work in the New Jerusalem and minister to those on the earth as "ministers of fire."[4] They also minister to God in worship. Daniel and John both saw an uncountable number of angels around the throne ministering to God. "Ten thousand times ten thousand" and "thousands of thousands" express an uncountable number. There could be hundreds of thousands or millions of angels in the throne room on the sea of glass at one time!

A thousand thousands ministered to Him; ten thousand times ten thousand stood before Him.—Daniel 7:10

Angels praise, thank, and discover God in worship alongside their brethren, the saints. Like us, they get to peer into the depths of God's glory and respond in fascinated worship. Daniel specifically said they minister to God, a priestly term for friendship with God through worship and prayer. No doubt, their songs and dance fill the atmosphere in heaven as they pour out their love for God.

And in the midst of the throne, and around the throne, were four living creatures full of eyes in front and in back….The four living creatures each having six wings, were full of eyes around and within. And they do not rest day or night, saying, "Holy, holy, holy, Lord God Almighty, who was and is and is to come!"—Revelation 4:6, 8

Within the realm of angels, there is a specific rank called the living creatures. Many people believe these are the same creatures that Isaiah saw above Jesus' throne.[5] Isaiah called them seraphim, which means "burning ones."[6] These four angelic beings are the ones closest to God's throne, and they help lead the entire throne room in worship. As

---

[4] Hebrews 1:14.

[5] Isaiah 6:2-4.

[6] Strong's Hebrew #08314 - https://www.studylight.org/lexicons/eng/hebrew/08314.html

they worship God, it releases the revelation of God to the elders, saints, and other angels, who then are inspired to respond with their worship.[7]

The living creatures are unique in that they have six wings, and their bodies are filled with eyes. John mentions their eyes two times to express their significance.

Their eyes are all around their bodies and wings, and even under their wings. God designed them to peer into His light with hundreds or thousands of eyes. They catch every angle of God's light as it hits them and moves in every direction around them in the room.

The worship of the creatures is unceasing. They gaze and proclaim without stopping, and they're never bored! Their worship is fueled by their ability to peer into the ocean of God's glory and experience fascination with all their eyes.

EXAMPLE IMAGES

I picture millions of angels standing on the sea of glass with me as I worship God. I imagine massive worship gatherings with celebratory music and dancing or massive prayer meetings with all those on the sea of glass singing prayers together. Then I picture tremendous waves of light spontaneously coming from God and passing through the masses of saints and angels in the throne room as they all respond with high praises or prostrate themselves on the sea of glass.

I picture large creatures flying around God's presence, gazing intently into His glory storm, and then singing out loud declarations of His beauty and His power. As I watch them, I listen to their loud proclamations of the beauty of God and watch the smoke of God's presence fill the room like in Isaiah's throne room scene. As they worship, I picture the room responding in worship from the inner circle working its way back in layers around the room.

EXAMPLE MEDITATION

Thousands upon thousands of angels on the sea of glass in Your presence! The place is filled with angels singing and dancing in Your glory. They minister to You in song.

I stand on the sea of glass with my brethren, the angels. I worship You with them by my side, Abba! Millions of saints and angels are singing and dancing in Your presence. They stand before You and minister to You in prayer and worship. This is the joyful gathering before the

---

7   Revelation 4:9, 5:8, 5:14.

God of the whole earth. Four living creatures that are full of eyes to see Your depths, experience You, and respond to You. Abba, You have designed these angels and set them right in front of You for a reason. You love it when Your creation sees Your beauty and is filled with fascination. They do not rest day or night flying around Your glory, shaking the heavenly temple with the thunder of their praise. Their eyes are filled with Your light. They see to the depths of You and never stop looking for more! A thousand eyes night and day for thousands of years could not exhaust the depths of the knowledge of God! I can hear the echo of their songs even now, and I can see the sanctuary responding row by row as far as the eye can see.

ELDERS AND SAINTS (REVELATION 4:4)

To the general assembly and church of the firstborn who are registered in heaven.—Hebrews 12:23

Around the throne are the saints who have died throughout history and are now with the Lord. Hebrews calls them the "church of the firstborn who are registered in heaven." They live in the New Jerusalem and get to enter the throne room to worship God face to face with no hindrances! Similar to the number of angels, the number of saints must be countless. These are real people; some are even our friends and family that get to experience God's full glory! Hebrews 12 says we come to the "festal assembly and church of the firstborn," which means the church gathers for festive, joyful celebrations in heaven.

When He opened the fifth seal, I saw under the altar the souls of those who had been slain for the word of God and for the testimony which they held. And they cried with a loud voice, saying, "How long O Lord, holy and true, until you judge and avenge our blood on those who dwell on the earth?"—Revelation 6:9-10

After these things I looked, and behold, a great multitude, which no one could number, of all nations, tribes, peoples, and tongues, standing before the Lamb clothed with white robes with palm branches in their hands, and crying out with a loud voice, "Salvation belongs to our God who sits on the throne, and to the Lamb."—Revelation 7:9-10

They gather to worship God face to face, pray for the nations of the earth, and receive direction from God in their assignments. The saints, angels, and living creatures are connected by the Holy Spirit and respond to one another's worship. They are robed in holy garments and minister to God as priests.

Out of the masses of saints, twenty-four real people are sitting on their thrones around God's throne. John calls them elders because they have a governmental position with Jesus. I believe twenty-four specific people sit next to God as His governing council as a part of their eternal rewards. But I think that they also give us a picture of our kingly position with Jesus in prayer and worship. Every believer has been joined to Jesus and His throne and has the privilege of partnering with Him in ruling His kingdom.

These elders are close to God, which reveals His desire for an intimate partnership. Like the living creatures, they gaze at God's beauty and respond in worship.[8] They are robed with beautiful garments and glorious crowns as a complete picture of what it looks like to be priestly kings. God's people rule and reign with Jesus by functioning as priests, including gazing on God, praying, and worshiping.

EXAMPLE IMAGES

I picture twenty-four men and women on these thrones with beautiful crowns on their heads and shining garments on their bodies. I picture their thrones encircling God's throne and facing Him. I imagine them looking into God's glory storm and falling on the ground in worship as the creatures praise Him. I listen for worship to go back and forth between the elders, saints, and angels, and I visualize them praying and agreeing with my prayers.

I set my mind on the throne room, and I picture myself in the same robe and crown on a governmental throne by God. I look at God face to face, and I speak my prayers and songs right to His heart. I take my place of governmental authority over the nations with Him on the elder's throne.

EXAMPLE MEDITATION

Twenty-four elders are sitting on twenty-four glorious thrones. God, You have ordained humanity to rule and reign with You for all of eternity. You set us right around Your throne to gaze

---

[8] Revelation 4:10, 5:8, 5:11, 5:14, 7:11, 11:16, 19:4.

on You and release Your power through prayer and worship. I sit on my throne on the sea of glass. I receive my robe and my crown, and I take my place of authority with You. I am a part of Your governing council. I get to make decisions with You in prayer and release Your plans in prayer.

WORSHIP IS A RESPONSE

Most believers want to experience genuine worship at the heart level and want to know how to cultivate it. To me, the key to growing in the heart of worship is seeing more of God. When we see more of God with our spiritual eyes, it naturally awakens wonder, praise, and thanksgiving. The living creatures have no problem flowing in worship at the heart level because they have eyes to see God and live from the place of discovery and fascination.

Worship can always be a choice when we're not feeling tender, but if worship is always only a choice, it's a sign of an unhealthy heart. True worship is a response to the revelation of God, and this is available to all of us. Stay before His bonfire, and genuine worship will continue to grow in your heart. Fascination will fill you and inspire songs and desire to flow like the living creatures.

WEEKLY ASSIGNMENT

Your first assignment this week is to take at least one prayer time to practice picturing the Biblical descriptions of God's glory storm. During your time, write down what you saw with your spiritual eyes, what you felt, and what you talked about with God. To get a rhythm in these descriptions, I encourage you to picture the throne room descriptions during all your prayer and worship times this week. The second assignment is to participate in one 30-minute group tongues time this week. During this time, the group should focus on picturing and meditating on one throne room description while praying in tongues. Intermittently, take turns speaking or singing out truths from the throne room description as they come to you. This prayer time should feel like a group meditation time.

DISCIPLESHIP MEETING GUIDE
MODULE 7: THRONE ROOM – CHAPTERS 30 & 31

MEETING FOCUS:

The purpose of this week's meeting is to discuss the value of God's beauty and process the meditation assignments.

DISCUSSION QUESTIONS (IN ORDER OF IMPORTANCE):

1. *Spiritual Pursuits*:
   a. Practically, how is your prayer schedule going? How many days have you walked out your prayer schedule? Do you need to make small changes to your schedule? How are your daily prayer times going, and how is God impacting you through them?

2. *Chapter Questions*:
   a. Chapter 30 – In-depth, share how your meditation time went.
   b. Chapter 31 – What are your thoughts and questions about the "holy fascination" and "worship is a response" sections of the chapter? In-depth, share how your meditation time went.

3. *Heart Issue*:
   a. Share how your heart issue has been going this past week. With heart issue discussions, process, confess, encourage, and pray together for God to release transformation. ***Pray in tongues together and ask God to release power to the heart issue.***

4. Briefly review the assignments for the next two weeks together. This is not necessary if you are having a group gathering to introduce the next module topic.

MEETING NOTES:

MODULE 8

FASTING

MODULE INTRODUCTION

For many people, the topic of fasting from food is either completely foreign, mystical, confusing, scary, or avoided. However, for those that long for God, fasting is a gift to bring them into the experience of His heart. In the physical weakness of fasting, there is an exponential tenderizing and awakening of desire for God that He then meets with the rivers of living waters.

When I got a vision for intimacy with God in college, I began weekly fasting and it grew the size of my heart. I began to touch God's heart, and those small experiences satisfied my growing thirst for more of Him. In each season where my desire is renewed or increased for nearness to God, I'm led to fast, and God satisfies me there.

Fasting is what your heart is longing for right now because your desire for Him has been increasing as you've been seeing His beauty and desire for you. He's been slowly awakening a longing for satisfaction and fascination in Him alone and fasting will soften your heart in a unique way. At some point, your desire will lead you to a place of wanting more of God, but you will feel like you've hit a plateau or spiritual wall. Fasting takes you past the wall and is the grace that escorts your heart into more intimacy with the Lord.

The purpose of this module is to give you a paradigm of fasting that is rooted in intimacy and longing for Jesus and equip you to fast weekly. The first chapter is focused on having a vision for intimacy with God in fasting. The last three chapters are geared towards preparing you in multiple ways for weekly fasting.

The assignments in this module will help you study and process the Biblical value of fasting and process your past experiences and perspectives on the topic. The practical assignments will help you think through what weekly fasting could look like for you, both now and in the future. There is no requirement to fast. Wherever you're at in your readiness or perspective on fasting, take this module to pray, study, and get more clarity on fasting to take one step forward.

ASSIGNMENT OVERVIEW
MODULE 8 – FASTING

Schedule a 1-3 day fast during week 39 to include extra prayer times within the fast. The details and examples to this are at the end of chapter 33. There is an extra Discipleship meeting during the last week to discuss practical ways to transition out of the curriculum.

Week Thirty-six Assignments:

❑ Read Chapter 32 – "**Lovesick Fasting.**" Journal your thoughts and questions about the chapter.

❑ Journal about your excitement, fears, past experiences, concerns, possible wrong motivations, and any hindrances with fasting from your life. This week, talk to God about each one.

❑ Begin fasting if you're ready.

❑ Fill out a new *Spiritual Pursuits Document* for this module. The pursuits can stay the same or change but filling out the form monthly helps you refocus and develop a rhythm of intentionality.

Week Thirty-seven Assignments:

❑ Read Chapter 33 – "**Weekly Fasting Part 1.**" Journal your thoughts and questions about the chapter.

❑ Continue journaling, processing, and praying through any heart issues related to fasting.

❑ Write down a rough draft plan for weekly fasting.

❑ Fast according to your plan if you're ready.

❑ **Meet with your Discipleship Mentor.**

Week Thirty-eight Assignments:

❑ Read Chapter 34 – "**Weekly Fasting Part 2.**" Journal your thoughts and questions about the chapter.

❑ Continue journaling, processing, and praying through any heart issues related to fasting.

❑ Finalize your weekly fasting plan.

❑ Fast this week if you're ready.

❑ As a group, schedule and plan the details of a 1-3-day fast with extra prayer times for next week.

Week Thirty-nine Assignments:

- ❑ Read Chapter 35 – "*Weekly Fasting Part 3.*" Journal your thoughts and questions about the chapter.
- ❑ Continue journaling, processing, and praying through any heart issues related to fasting.
- ❑ Complete the 1–3-day group fast.
- ❑ **Meet with your Discipleship Mentor.**

Week Forty Assignments:

- ❑ Read Chapter 36 – *"Transition Week."* Journal your thoughts and questions about the chapter.
- ❑ Complete the *Transition Assignment* in preparation for your Discipleship Mentor meeting.
- ❑ Fast this week if you're ready.
- ❑ **Meet with your Discipleship Mentor.**

As you begin this module on fasting, I need to give a clear disclaimer: I am not a doctor nor a nutritionist. My suggestions are coming from my experience and from fasting research I have done, but I encourage you to do more research and talk to your doctor and nutritionist in your own journey. Also, if you have struggled with body image issues and eating disorders, it would be wise to talk to your doctor and pastor to help discern if and when fasting could be healthy for you.

SPIRITUAL PURSUITS   DATE: _____

1. **Bible reading direction and plan**
   (Write down what you will read and when you will read it):

2. **Meditation verse** (Choose a verse that speaks truth into your heart issue):

3. **Sin/character issue from which to get freedom:**

4. **Lie from which to pursue deliverance:**

5. **Gifting to pursue** (Include simple ways you can pursue it):

Weekly Prayer Schedule—Write down your plan for the *specific times* you are committed to spending with God each day, and *what specifically you plan to do during those times*. Include what your study or meditation focus will be. Refer to the example schedule in Chapter Two. (e.g., Monday 6-6:30 am—Tongues, 6:30-7:30 am—Meditation on Song of Solomon 1:2)

Monday

Tuesday

Wednesday

Thursday

Friday

Saturday

Sunday

32

LOVESICK FASTING

▌INTIMACY PARADIGM - MATTHEW 9

In Matthew 9:14-17, Jesus unveiled a new paradigm of fasting motivated out of longing for His nearness as the intimate Bridegroom. In context to these verses, Jesus knew He would be leaving His friends physically, and He knew that they would long for His nearness and friendship during His absence. Because of this, He gave them the gift of fasting as the doorway into the experience of His nearness in the Spirit. This intimacy paradigm, combined with the dynamic experience of God's heart in fasting, is the new wineskin that Jesus wanted His friends to grab onto as they formed the DNA of the early church.

The world, and some in the church, see fasting mostly as abstaining from food and legitimate pleasures, but Jesus sees fasting as feasting in the realm of the Spirit. Fasting is saying no to small and momentary pleasures unto drinking of the superior pleasures of God's heart. Fasting doesn't prove anything or earn anything from God, but it does posture our spirit, soul, and body to look for another source of life. When we posture our hearts towards Him instead of food in a prolonged way, something dynamic happens—God awakens longing inside us and satisfies us with His manifest presence.

JOHN'S DISCIPLES

Then the disciples of John came to Him, saying, "Why do we and the Pharisees fast often, but Your disciples do not fast?"—Matthew 9:14

Jesus' teaching begins as the disciples of John the Baptist come to Him to ask about fasting. They fasted often, and so did the Pharisees, which was probably two days a week.[1] Somehow, they knew that Jesus' disciples didn't fast, and they wanted to know why. It is significant that the people asking Jesus the question were John's disciples because we know that they agreed with John's values and that John had a revelation of God's value for fasting. So, we have to assume John and his disciples understood the dynamic role of fasting in God's kingdom.

John was the greatest prophet ever born and was extravagant in his fasting and intimacy with God. He was spiritually violent and aggressive in his pursuit of the Lord, and Jesus called him a "burning and shining lamp" that released God's light to his generation.[2] John exemplified the fasted lifestyle and its benefits by living in the wilderness away from the comforts and distractions of his day. Instead, he chose to feast on God in fasting, prayer, and meditation on the Word until the day of his appearing as a prophet.[3] In his season of ministry preparation, John encountered the voice of Jesus as the passionate Bridegroom, and he was filled with all joy in his prayer times.[4] Needless to say, fasting was core to John's relationship with God, and the supernatural fruit was evident!

We see John's ministry, heart and how Jesus defined him in the scriptures, so when we read about his disciples, we must understand they owned and lived out John's values for fasting. They approached Jesus and asked about fasting because it was something John taught them to care about. Can you imagine the stories John shared with his disciples about fasting and encountering God? He had years of testimonies in the wilderness in preparation to be the sole person equipped to prepare Israel for God's coming in the flesh. John's testimonies inspired his disciples and caused them to follow him in the fasted lifestyle.

---

[1] Luke 18:12.
[2] Matthew 9:11-14; John 5:35.
[3] Luke 3:2.
[4] John 3:29.

Undoubtedly, up until their meeting with Jesus, they had fasted with John and encountered God for themselves. I don't assume they were religious and legalistic in their approach. I believe they touched God's heart in fasting and did it often because John gave them a high vision for intimacy with God. John had an intense message for the nation, so anyone who would associate with him and follow him in his message and lifestyle would have been hungry and wholehearted in their relationship with God.

LONGING FOR THE BRIDEGROOM

And Jesus said to them, "Can the friends of the bridegroom mourn as long as the bridegroom is with them? But the days will come when the bridegroom will be taken away from them, and then they will fast.—Matthew 9:15

John's disciples came to Jesus with their question because they cared deeply about fasting and intimacy with God. They were sincerely perplexed with the disciples' lack of fasting and wanted insight. Jesus responded to their spiritual hunger by giving them the greatest revelation of fasting He had ever taught, one which would reveal His core identity and desire.

Jesus revealed His identity as a Bridegroom who desired a bride. He is burning with eternal passion and longing for deep friendship and union with one that is made in His image. This is what He longed and burned for in the creation story. In Genesis 1, God saw that every creature had another one made in its likeness for friendship and fruitfulness, and He desired the same oneness with one made in His image. Jesus is a Bridegroom looking for a bride to lavish His love on and receive wholehearted love from. In this story, Jesus connected fasting with marital love and His desire to encounter us with love.

Jesus said that His disciples didn't need to fast because He was physically with them already. This reveals that the purpose of fasting is to experience God's manifest presence. In Jesus, the disciples had the fullness of God around them all the time. He experienced their friendship, and they experienced Him, so it wasn't necessary to fast for the sake of intimacy.

Then Jesus prophesied and said that a day was coming when He wouldn't be with His disciples anymore. In that day of physical absence, they would end up fasting often like John's disciples. In that day, they would come into the purpose of fasting, which is to experience deep friendship with God in His presence.

Jesus understood that His disciples would fast out of a lovesick desire for His nearness. Lovesickness is an emotion of love and passion for someone so strong that it makes you sick emotionally. There's a real pain and groaning with awakened yet unsatisfied longing. To be lovesick is to be fully surrendered to the longing for intimacy with Him to the point that you're taken over by longing and consumed until the longing is satisfied. Jesus knew His friends would be addicted to His presence after years of walking with Him. He knew their hearts would be ravished with love after experiencing such nearness and that they would do anything to feel that intimacy again during His physical absence.

Think about what they experienced in just a few years of walking with him. Their eyes saw the fullness of God's personality manifested in a human frame! They got to look at Jesus and see the details and color of His eyes, the curves and wrinkles of His cheeks, His facial expressions, and His mannerisms. Jesus is the happy God, so they also saw His smile, heard His unique laugh, and sang and danced with Him in worship. Daily, they talked to Him and listened to the subtle intonations and fluctuations of His voice. With their own ears, they heard Jesus say their names and say what He loved about them.

The disciples looked into the eyes of the Psalm 139 God who searched them, knew them, thought about them more than the sands of the sea, and burned with passion for them. They didn't just meditate on Psalm 139—they experienced it face to face with Jesus. How would you feel if God was standing next to you and knew every detail about your inner workings yet still probed you and searched out your heart in conversation? How understood, accepted, and enjoyed would you feel if He never left because of your sin and weakness but continually prophesied His love and your destiny over you? How content and satisfied would you be? This love is what His friends experienced for three years while walking with Him, and this is what ruined them for anything less.

While He was with them, He satisfied the God-given longings within each one of His friends. Then He gave them fasting as the means to experiencing that same presence by the Spirit in His absence. For the disciples, fasting became feasting on the presence of Jesus in their place of prayer. The One that they longed to hear, and see, and touch again was found in the time of fasting as God's gift to them.

NEW WINESKINS FOR HIS PRESENCE

Nor do they put new wine into old wineskins, or else the wineskins break, the wine is spilled, and the wineskins are ruined. But they put new wine into new wineskins and both are preserved.—Matthew 9:17

There are two pictures that Jesus gives to express what fasting does to the human heart. Both point to the renewing and tenderizing effect that fasting has on us. The first picture is of an unshrunk cloth being put on an old garment, and the second picture of new wine being poured into an old wineskin. In both scenarios, the new item isn't compatible with the old, and when they are put together, the old item is ruined.

When an unshrunk cloth is attached to an old garment that has been shrunk, it rips the fabric when it eventually shrinks. The idea is that the old garment isn't able to steward the new material. Likewise, the new wine wasn't compatible with old wineskins. New wine had to be put in a new skin because, over time, the wine would ferment, which would cause the skin to expand. Pouring new wine into an already expanded wineskin would cause it to stretch beyond its capacity, causing it to break open and pour out the wine.

Some commentators will say that Jesus used these pictures to say that His disciples shouldn't fast in the new covenant because it's unnecessary and people can't handle it. In this perspective, fasting is the old cloth and wineskin, which are incompatible with Jesus' disciples and those in the new covenant. I believe Jesus is saying the opposite. His point is that fasting with the intimacy perspective is the new wineskin lifestyle that can handle the new wine of His presence as the Bridegroom. Within this intimacy perspective, it's the fasted lifestyle that flows out of longing for God that tenderizes and expands the heart so that it can be a container for greater levels of God's manifest presence.

The fasted lifestyle and the expanded heart, combined with encountering Jesus as Bridegroom, is the spiritual infrastructure that Jesus wanted to sow into the early church. He sought to wound His friends with a deep and penetrating love so that they'd have a high vision for encounter through fasting during His absence and disciple others in the same vision. Jesus wanted the grace of fasting and the value of encountering Him as the Bridegroom God to saturate the church so that the first and greatest commandment would always be honored.

SUMMARY

Matthew 9 is the first time Jesus self-identifies as the Bridegroom, which is critical to understand. Jesus' identity and His desires are the central themes of this teaching. Why? Because He wants us to know that He is a Bridegroom God who has an infinite desire for friendship and union with His bride. God is burning for us! He created us out of a pure and burning longing and then died for us with the same heartbeat. Now He desires to share His thoughts and emotions with   us as His bride through tangible encounters with His presence. God wants us to experience His heart and His nearness, and He wants to feel our love for Him. He is rich in love and pleasures, and His heart is to saturate our being with Him and display His glory to us![5] I believe that He desires to fascinate and satisfy us so that we live out of the overflow of fulfilled longings.

Though there may be a mountain of unbelief in some hearts regarding God's desire to encounter and satisfy, God's heart is to give us the fullness of His life.

His invitation to abide in the vine of His love and joy and drink from the river of His presence is always open to those who thirst and desire for more of God. *"And let him who thirsts come. Whoever desires, let him take the water of life freely."*[6] God burns with desire for us to be rooted and grounded in the experience of His nearness and to be filled with the fullness of God as we encounter the depth, width, length, and height of His love for us.[7]

In God's heart, fasting is deeply knit to experiencing His love as the Bridegroom. It prepares the fabric of our hearts to encounter and then contain God's love. It supernaturally tenderizes us like a new wineskin and then expands the size of our hearts to experience Him even more. Fasting is a supernatural grace from God that transforms and prepares our hearts for a greater union with God as Bridegroom.

▌ INTIMACY BENEFITS WITH FASTING

This section needs to be prefaced with the statement that every person will experience differing levels of these benefits during fasting. The differing factors are your history of fasting, amount of time fasting, amount of time spent with God on a fast, everyday lifestyle, and God's leadership. Overall, God is doing something personal in

---

[5] John 17:24.

[6] Revelation 22:17; John 15:9-11.

[7] Ephesians 3:16-19.

each person's life, so He knows what to release and what to delay in accordance with His long-term purpose in us.

History of fasting refers to someone's investment in fasting. If they've been fasting consistently, the benefits add up and the experience probably increases. The amount of time of fasting, whether it's one meal or two days, influences the experience in the same way that spending more time in prayer increases the experience. It's possible to fast without necessarily spending more time with God, so if you schedule more time with Him during fasting, more seeds will be sown in your heart. The last factor is lifestyle choices. What you sow into (flesh or spirit) as a lifestyle on non-fasting days will add to or detract from your fasting benefits. With this preface in mind, let the testimony of these benefits stir your heart with expectation!

LONGING FOR GOD

Fasting is an expression of longing for God, and it intensifies our longing for God. It's an expression of longing in that we choose to say no to legitimate needs and pleasures out of a desire for more of God. When we fast, we create more time and space for Him to be our source instead of other things. This is all birthed out of desire and longing for God.

While fasting, longing intensifies for two reasons. One is that when we're not eating, entertaining ourselves, or distracting ourselves, our longings are not pacified or wrongly satisfied. When they're not satisfied, they are allowed to grow and intensify like hunger pains that grow within us until we eat. Hunger pains are our bodies telling us what they need and motivating us to pursue food. Spiritual longings are like hunger pains, and they intensify to tell us to seek God until satisfied. Awakened longings motivate us to pursue God!

Longings also intensify while fasting because they are overwhelmingly satisfied in God's presence and begin to demand more of Him. Encounters with God's presence satisfy, and at the same time, they increase longing for more and more of Him. True intimacy with God births a deeper longing to be with and know Him in greater ways. *Longing and love are meant to grow.* Once we begin to experience more of God in fasting, satisfaction and longing will grow and motivate us to keep fasting. We choose to fast when there is a small amount of desire in us, but God will birth new levels of desire in us in the context of fasting and intimacy with Him.

TENDERNESS AND CONNECTEDNESS

Through fasting, the Holy Spirit transforms and prepares the fabric of hearts to be compatible with the new wine of God's presence. The main point from Jesus' fasting teaching is that those who prepare their hearts through fasting will experience His affections as the Bridegroom. This tenderizing effect results in a multiplied sensitivity to God's presence, a deeper sense of emotional connectedness to God, and flowing emotions of love. I want to be careful not to exaggerate or hype things up, but my experience and those I've run with prove that fasting multiplies our spiritual experience with God.

These experiences are real and change everything. This intimacy is the reward of fasting and validates the truth that God is the highest pleasure available to the human heart! Often, my emotions are awakened and overflow with gentle tears or weeping as I feel the love of God wash over me. During meditation, I experience gentle waves of His presence come upon my body. When I read the Bible and worship, my thoughts experience levels of fascination and excitement as the Spirit enlightens my eyes to His truths.

Last, the increased awareness of His presence in me produces a real sense of oneness and connectedness with God as a person. I would describe connectedness as a consistent flow of thoughts and emotions between God's heart and my heart. This connectedness is tangible.

EXPANDED HEART SIZE

Like the new wineskin imagery from Jesus' teaching, our hearts are containers for God's manifest presence, and they can expand and grow. Fasting and encounters with God work something in our hearts to increase their size. When our hearts grow, longing grows, pursuit grows, and the measure of His presence that we can experience grows. This means that your heart can steward more of God's glory in an encounter. The larger the wineskin, the greater the amount of wine it can contain at a time.

That He would grant you, according to the riches of His glory, to be strengthened with might through His Spirit in the inner man, that Christ may dwell in your hearts through faith; that you, being rooted and grounded in love, may be able to comprehend with all the saints what is the width and length and depth and height - to know the love of Christ which passes knowledge.
—Ephesians 3:16-19

Paul's prayer in Ephesians 3 tells us that our hearts can increase in their capacity to contain God's presence. First, he prays for the Holy Spirit to strengthen the inner man (the heart) with supernatural glory. When the Spirit strengthens our inner man with might, He enlarges our hearts' capacity to experience God's presence. The fruit of a strengthened heart is that Jesus' presence will increase and dwell there in a manifest way. As the Spirit enlarges our hearts with might and Jesus' manifest presence increases in us, we are prepared for greater experiences with the heights and depths of His love. Fasting positions our hearts to be strengthened and enlarged by the Spirit to experience the depths of God's love.

ASK FOR LOVESICKNESS

No matter where you're at in your experience and understanding of fasting, the most appropriate response to this chapter is to bow down at Jesus' feet and ask Him to touch you with holy longing. Pray for a longing to know His heart and affections as the Bridegroom in such a way that would cause you to fast out of lovesickness. God wants to renew your desire for Him and fasting, and He wants to heal any wrong perspectives, motivations, and bad experiences you've had. He wants to give you fresh hope that you can feel His affection for you in your thoughts and emotions through the tenderizing grace that fasting brings. I know that the topic of fasting can bring up a multitude of questions, fears, and hesitations, but be slow to disqualify yourself from the grace of fasting. When hope and desire take root, you will find your way in all of this—just start by inviting Him to move on your heart.

WEEKLY ASSIGNMENT

This week, take some time to journal your thoughts on fasting. Write down what excites you, what fears and concerns you have, what possible wrong motivations you've had, and any past experiences (positive or negative) you've had with fasting. While processing these things, talk to God about each one so that you're better prepared to practice fasting the next few weeks. If you know you're ready to fast or already fast consistently, begin considering what the next step in fasting might be for you.

33

WEEKLY FASTING PART ONE

MY JOURNEY

God has washed and transformed me in the place of fasting. I've been so impacted by my past seasons of consistent weekly fasting and specific extended fasts that I still look back on them when I need fresh hope and vision for intimacy with God. I'm almost twenty years into living out the fasted lifestyle, and I'm deeply convinced that fasting is available and critical for every believer to go deeper in God. From experience, I can say that it's a catalyst for God's activity in the human heart.

When I was twenty years old in college, my dad inspired me to go on a fast. My first fast ever, and I decided to do a 40-day fast! I had no clue what to do in the fast except to pray during my regular mealtimes so that God could be my sustenance. It was a "liquid" fast, which for me at that time meant instant breakfast shakes, milk, and juice. Not the healthiest way to fast, but it worked that time around. Needless to say, I broke my fast after seven days, but God met me, and it was sacred to me. I can still tell you the exact dates of that fast and all that God did to me. I experienced His presence in many of those alone times, which was newer for me. The Bible came alive, and I felt my desires for God increase in that one week. That's also when I received the infilling of the Holy Spirit, prayed in tongues, and began receiving prophetic impressions!

After that experience, I began fasting one day a week with two friends. Those fasting days were always special and set apart for more time with God, and what God did in that year set my spiritual foundation for the things to come. My milestone experiences with God happened the same year that I started fasting, and it helped me go as deep as I could in my early twenties.

My weekly fasting was strengthened when I went to Bible school, where fasting was taught and modeled right in front of me by leaders who had a long history of the fruitfulness of fasting. In my time there, I wanted to fast more often but was rarely able to until my third and fourth year in Bible school. Corey Russell led a program that many of my friends decided to join, including my future wife. In the program, we committed to fast together (1-3 days) weekly and share life daily in small groups and the prayer room. We touched a grace to fast that I had never experienced, and the interior fruit was undeniable.

During these two years, I first began to experience near-daily tears when reading the Bible and praying as God's presence touched me. On some days, just whispering one phrase from a verse would be enough for my heart to move and His presence to swirl inside of me. The exponential fruit of experiencing God in fasting in that two-year season convinced me that the inconveniences and challenges of fasting long-term were well worth it.

At various times, I draw back from fasting or break my weekly fast early because of a lack of vision, discouragement, dullness, an unhealthy dependency on food, or just physical weariness from life. But I quickly notice the diminished heart tenderness, and sign back up for fasting. Every time I say yes again, I'm surprised by how much He touches me and washes away dullness and discouragement.

FASTING DEFINED

By definition, fasting is abstaining from food in some way, whether limiting eating to certain foods or only taking in liquids. There are other legitimate and fruitful ways to fast, like turning off social media and entertainment for a time but abstaining from food is the core expression and type of fasting I encourage people to step into. Fasting is turning our attention away from our physical needs and appetites to focus on our spirit-man's needs and appetites. The purpose of fasting is to feast on superior and eternal pleasures instead of inferior and temporary pleasures.

WEAKNESS PERSPECTIVE

And He said to me, "My grace is sufficient for you, for My strength is made perfect in weakness." Therefore most gladly I will rather boast in my infirmities, that the power of Christ may rest upon me. Therefore I take pleasure in infirmities, in reproaches, in needs, in persecutions, in distresses, for Christ's sake. For when I am weak, then I am strong.—2 Corinthians 12:9-10

In God's kingdom, there is an unusual principle that Paul explains in 2 Corinthians 12. The principle is that God releases more supernatural power to believers when they are positioned in certain kinds of weakness. God's strength is made perfect in the midst of human weakness, and Jesus' power rests on those who choose the foolish and weak ways of the kingdom. Paul was weak in the sense that he was attacked by demons, persecuted, shipwrecked, hungry and sleepless at times, and in fastings often.[1] He had circumstances, and he made lifestyle decisions that put him at a disadvantage in the natural realm. Paul pleaded with Jesus to remove the thorn in his flesh in three different seasons before Jesus visited him and explained this principle.

After Jesus' visitation, Paul boasted in the circumstances and lifestyle choices that made him weak and dependent on God because he understood that the Spirit increased on him more in that posture. Paul knew that he was positioned to be made strong and mighty in the Spirit when he was weak. This principle completely contradicts the ways of the world!

Fasting is meant to be seen within this principle: it's a weakness that we choose in order to have God's Spirit rest on us. Paul had many weaknesses that were not voluntary, but he did choose to fast, and he often fasted to access God's power.

How is fasting a weakness? When you're not eating, you have less energy to accomplish things in your strength. When you can't accomplish what you need to, you should naturally end up with less money, less pleasure, and less of a reputation. And if you're fasting, you're probably spending more time in prayer, which makes it even worse. Time and energy are what we need to make our lives and our dreams work out, right? This is true in the marketplace but also in ministry. Suppose pastors give time and energy to fasting

---

[1] 2 Corinthians 11:24-28, 12:7-10.

and prayer. In that case, they are choosing not to do things that would build up their ministries like counseling sessions, extra admin meetings, networking, developing skills, marketing, and evangelism.

When we fast food and give extra time to prayer, we are positioning ourselves in physical and mental weakness knowing that God's manifest strength will be perfected in us and on us. His strength doesn't just mean the power to endure a fast. It refers to God's presence, encounters, supernatural tenderizing of our emotions, increased heart size, revelation in the Word, His activity through us in gifts of the Spirit, and Him making areas of our lives fruitful. God's power on us is multi-dimensional, and God more than makes up for "lost time" in fasting and prayer!

In the Sermon on the Mount, Jesus taught on the same principle. In Matthew 6, He highlighted five different postures of weakness that position us to receive more of His power. In context to the entire teaching of Matthew 5-7, His power breaks sin patterns and brings the human heart into the happiness of the beatitudes. The five areas of weakness are: serving others with good works, praying, forgiving and blessing our enemies, fasting, and giving money away. In his book, *The Rewards of Fasting,* Mike Bickle explains how each of the five expressions brings us into a place of natural weakness.

Jesus set forth these five activities as foundational to the Kingdom of God. By giving, we fast our money and financial strength. In serving and prayer, we are fasting our time and energy, investing it in others and in intercession. Blessing our enemies requires that we fast our words and reputation. In giving up food, we are fasting our physical and emotional strength.[2]

WEEKLY FASTING

My encouragement to you, no matter where you are in your journey, is to consider fasting weekly. Yes, long fasts are amazing and appear to be more radical but think of a weekly lifestyle when you think of fasting. If you're newer to fasting, consider one meal or one day a week of some fast (liquid or partial) and a three-day fast every few months. If you're more experienced and have the desire, consider fasting one to two days a week and adding in a three-day fast every couple months. Some version of weekly

---

[2] Bickle, Mike, and Dana Candler. 2005. *The Rewards of Fasting: Experiencing the Power and Affections of God* (Kansas City, MO: Forerunner Books), 71.

fasting is doable and beneficial for every person in every season and creates a sustainable physical and spiritual rhythm.

I began my fasting journey in college by fasting one day a week, which lasted for a few years. Halfway through Bible school, I increased to two days a week while substituting in a three-day fast every month or two. At IHOP-KC, there is a corporate three-day fast every month on the first Monday through Wednesday that people worldwide join in on. Most times, I jumped into that corporate rhythm, and it really blessed me. My long-term vision is to make that three-day fast a part of my monthly rhythm before the Lord. The fast is called the Global Bridegroom Fast, and IHOP-KC hosts it every month. I encourage you to learn more about it to see if you'd like to participate in that.

PRACTICAL BENEFITS

There are many benefits to weekly fasting. First, it is doable and sustainable both physically and spiritually. I think most believers can do long fasts, but shorter weekly fasts are easier to say yes to and navigate. Second, weekly fasting helps develop a whole life rhythm of prayer, diet, and exercise. Fasting adds a unique but good pressure to think through how each area can flow together in harmony. Simply put, you can't eat unhealthily and not exercise and expect to fast every week while feeling its benefits. If you only do long fasts, you change your life rhythm for a short window of time, but then, potentially, you revert to your old rhythms. Weekly fasts keep you in focus every week, and they allow your heart and body to adapt. In the same way that our bodies adapt and respond to regular exercise, our hearts and bodies adapt to fasting when it's done consistently. When I have a good fasting rhythm, I feel like my mind and body know my fasting days and kick into fasting mode.

The third benefit is that the small tenderizing effects of fasting days can carry over to the other days of the week. Paul said that God's power "rested" on him in His weakness. God's power will "rest" or remain on you on non-fasting days if you have a weekly posture of weakness. Along with the carry-over effect, the weekly tenderizing benefits will gradually build up month after month.

BIBLICAL AND HISTORICAL EXAMPLES

There is significant precedence for weekly fasting in the Bible and throughout church history, giving us courage and confidence. It was usual for some Pharisees in

Jesus' day to voluntarily fast two days a week (Monday and Thursday).[3] Jesus didn't say their fasting was wrong, and He didn't rebuke every Pharisee. In one parable, He compared the potential self-righteous heart with an honest heart in Luke 18:12; this addresses the individual heart more than the act of fasting.

John's disciples fasted often and referenced the fasting of the Pharisees, which makes me think John and his disciples also fasted two days a week. Anna the prophetess, "Served God with fastings and prayers night and day."[4] The language of her fasting seems like it was consistent and even weekly for decades. You better believe Anna found a sustainable rhythm in fasting to be able to do it that long!

The first-century Church adapted the Pharisee's rhythm and fasted on Wednesdays and Fridays.[5] The early church fasting rhythm shows that Jesus' disciples valued two days of fasting and reinforces the belief that John and his disciples did as well. Paul lived out the same fasting value by fasting for three days at his conversion, fasting with others for direction, fasting when commissioning new elders, and fasting "often" in his life.[6]

Revolutionary Church leaders modeled fasting throughout history. To mention a few, Martin Luther, John Knox, John Calvin, John Wesley, and Charles Finney were aggressive fasters. Martin Luther was against the false doctrines in the Catholic Church, but he understood fasting as a grace in God's kingdom and fasted so much that he was criticized by those who didn't understand grace. John Knox and John Calvin, both global revivalists after Luther, were mighty in spirit because of their commitment to fasting. It's said that Calvin fasted until the city of Geneva was in revival and that the Queen feared Knox's prayer and fasting more than enemy armies.[7]

John Wesley, a father of the 1st Great Awakening in America and Europe, fasted two days a week and only commissioned leaders who would fast two days a week and pray

---

3 Julius Greenstone, Emil Hirsch, Hartwig Hirschfelf, "Fasting and Fasting Days." Jewish Encyclopedia online.
   https://www.jewishencyclopedia.com/articles/6033-fasting-and-fast-days

4 Luke 2:37.

5 Thomas Turrants, "The Place of Fasting in the Christian Life," *Knowing and Doing Magazine,* Summer of 2018. https://www.cslewisinstitute.org/The_Place_of_Fasting_in_the_Christian_Life_ FullArticle Allen, George Cantrell, *The Didache* (London: Astolat Press, 1903) 8:1.

6 Acts 9:9, 13:2-3, 14:23; 2 Corinthians 6:5, 11:27.

7 Toni Cauchi, "Let's Put Fasting Back on the Table." https://www.revivallibrary.org/resources/ revival_researchers/newsletter_articles/lets_put_fasting_back_on_menu.shtml

two hours a day like he did. Charles Finney shook America with preaching that pierced hearts in the 2nd Great Awakening, leading to hundreds of thousands coming to Jesus in radical ways. Frequently, he would fast Friday through Sunday before preaching or fast for days when he felt the spirit of prayer decrease in his heart and the spirit of power decrease in his preaching.[8] Lest we have a low vision of what he called powerful preaching, it was common for unbelievers to groan and weep under the conviction of the Spirit during his preaching before they fully surrendered their hearts to God.

HOW TO FAST WEEKLY

This section is a basic introduction of things to think about or be aware of as you pray about fasting weekly. In the next chapter, we'll look at each of these areas in more detail. Thinking about these things will help you fast more consistently, and it will make your fasting times more intentional and sacred.

PLAN THE DETAILS

Begin preparing for weekly fasting by deciding what type of fast you'll be doing. Based on that, think through what you would need to buy or prepare ahead of time. There are four main types of weekly fasts to consider.[9] Each of them is doable for most people, but they offer different amounts of energy based on your health or life situation.

1. *Water fast* – This is limited to water or other liquids that do not provide calories or energy. Most people can do a water fast for part of a day or an entire day, but there is significantly less energy than the other fasts.

2. *Liquid fast* – This includes light fruit or vegetable juices (not blended smoothies) or other liquids that don't contain fats, proteins or require the stomach to work hard. The benefit of a liquid fast is that it allows the body and digestive system to rest while still having a good amount of energy. The liquid fast is my "go-to" fast. It works with ministry responsibilities and the demands of young children, and I can determine my energy levels by how much juice I drink.

3. *Partial or Daniel fast* – This fast includes eating small portions of light foods like nuts and vegetables. Daniel mentions fasting on only vegetables in his

---

[8] Ibid.
[9] Bickle, *The Rewards of Fasting*, 77-78.

early teenage years in Babylon.[10] In his elderly years, he mentions fasting twenty-one days with no pleasant foods, meats, or wine.[11] The Daniel fast is a legitimate fast! The idea is to eat small enough portions so that your body can still rest, and you can experience the strength of God while having enough energy for the day.

4. *Benedict fast* – Named after Saint Benedict, a leader in the monastic movement during the 6th century, this fast includes eating only one meal a day and water or liquids for the other meals. Like the Daniel fast, this is very sustainable yet touches the heart and benefits of fasting.

Next, choose your fasting day or days and what specific meals you plan on skipping. What time of the week works the best for you to have a little less energy? What days allow you to spend more time with the Lord while fasting? Do you have other weekly commitments you want to plan around?

CONSECRATION PLAN

To consecrate something means to make it sacred and set apart from ordinary life. How can you make your time sacred and different from the other days of the week when you fast? Making it sacred could include planning extra prayer time and avoiding media, entertainment, recreational activities, unintentional hangouts, and other natural stimulants. You could also write down a vision sentence for your fasting times and write down any specific prayers you want to focus on consistently. As a sacred time with the Lord, prioritize fulfilling your fasting and prayer commitments, even when other things come up.

PHYSICAL PREPARATION

This will take a little time to research, and we'll get into more details in the next chapter, but you will need to think through how to prepare your body to go into and come out of your fasting times. Preparation mostly comes down to what you eat for one or two meals before and after a fasting day to acclimate your body. But this also includes learning

---

[10] Daniel 1:8-21.
[11] Daniel 10:2-3.

how your body responds to fasting and establishing a healthy lifestyle of exercise and diet that help facilitate healthy long-term fasting.

CHALLENGES

There are many areas of challenge that go with the fasted lifestyle. Physically, there is a measure of detoxification, depending on your regular diet, that can make fasting uncomfortable or discouraging. You will have less energy, but you will have to push through to fulfill your life responsibilities. Emotionally, dullness and barrenness will be more exposed when other stimulants aren't an option. God will meet you in needy emotions, but there is a painful transition that will take time. Relationally, friends or family may not understand or support your decision to fast. Spiritually, the enemy will try to discourage you or distract you from fasting because he knows how powerful it is in the spiritual realm. You may even face the challenge of seeing your wrong motivations in fasting.

YOU CAN FAST!

Whether you have been fasting for years or this is the first time you've considered fasting, I want to declare that you can fast! Fasting is not for super Christians, and it's not for the "next season" that's hopefully easier, because that may or may not come. It's doable in this season, and God's powerful grace will touch you and tenderize you. There are real challenges, but God will help you conquer them like He's empowered you to overcome other things. Besides, all the challenges pale in comparison to the experience of the glory of God in fasting.

If you feel a lack of desire for God and fasting, continue to ask Him to give you the gift of desire until you feel it flowing in your emotions. If you want to fast but have fears or don't know how, start small like one meal a week, and go from there each week. God will lead you, and you'll overcome the fears that come with the unknown realities of fasting.

WEEKLY ASSIGNMENT

This week, take some time to write down your fasting desires and draft a realistic plan for weekly fasting. *Questions to answer: (1) What day/meal(s) will you fast? (2) What kind of fast will you do? (3) How long will it last? (4) When would you pray? (5) How will you prepare food-wise? (i.e., what will be your last meal, and what will you break your fast with?)*

You will refine your plans as an assignment for each chapter, so there is time to work them out.

If you're ready to fast according to your plan during this week, journal your thoughts, challenges (physical, emotional, etc.), and experiences from the fast. Reflecting will help you recognize any fasting benefits. It will also help you refine your fasting plans because you'll learn ways to steward your body and schedule from your experience.

There is no expectation as to how much you should fast. I suggest starting with a liquid or partial fast one day a week, but you could fast one to two meals if that's easier. There's no rush to fast more than what you're ready for. There's grace and lots of time, and you can be confident that if you take one more step into fasting, God will fill you and lead you into more grace for fasting long-term.

DISCIPLESHIP MEETING GUIDE
MODULE 8: FASTING – CHAPTERS 32 & 33

MEETING FOCUS:

The purpose of this meeting is to discuss your level of desire for fasting, process fears, and hindrances, and work on a weekly fasting plan.

DISCUSSION QUESTIONS: (IN ORDER OF IMPORTANCE)

1. ***Spiritual Pursuits:***
    a. Practically, how is your prayer schedule going? How many days have you walked out your prayer schedule? Do you need to make small changes to your schedule? How are your daily prayer times going, and how is God impacting you through them?
    b. Briefly review your new *Spiritual Pursuits Document*.

2. ***Chapter Questions:***
    a. Chapter 32 – Discuss any of your journaled thoughts and questions from the chapter. Have you had an intimacy paradigm of fasting before?
    b. Prayer Assignment - What are your experiences with fasting? What fears do you have concerning weekly fasting, and does anything excite you about it?
    c. Chapter 33 – Discuss any of your journaled thoughts and questions from the chapter. What are the most helpful practical questions you have about fasting? In-depth, discuss your rough draft fasting plans.

3. ***Heart Issue:***
    a. Share how your heart issue has been going this past week. With heart issue discussions, process, confess, encourage, and pray together for God to release transformation. ***Pray in tongues together and ask God to release power to the heart issue.***

4. Briefly review the assignments for the next two weeks together.

MEETING NOTES:

34

WEEKLY FASTING PART TWO

INTRODUCTION

In the previous chapter, I introduced an outline of things to be aware of and think through with weekly fasting. In this chapter, we're going to go much deeper into what fasting can look like and feel like to help prepare you for what you want to step into in this season. Thinking about these things will help you fast more consistently, because it will prepare you spiritually and physically, and it will help you to overcome fasting challenges when they come. Your fasting times will feel more intentional and sacred like you are "entering into" a holy fast each week. The more thought you put into your fasting times, the more ownership and commitment you will have.

I'm writing from my experience in fasting, what I've learned from others, and what I've gleaned in reading books on fasting. In saying that, your experiences or challenges with fasting might be different in some ways. You will need to journal your experiences and observe how your soul and body respond to fasting over the years to understand and steward fasting in your life.

I highly recommend reading fasting and nutrition books. They will help you better understand how your body responds to fasting and what diet and exercise should look like to best steward the fasted lifestyle. Example books to read are *The Miracle of Fasting* by Patricia and Paul Bragg, *The Complete Guide to Fasting* by Dr. Jason Fung and Jimmy Moore, and *Fasting God's Way* by Sam Quartey.

▐ PLAN THE DETAILS

SCHEDULE FASTING TIMES

Begin planning the details of your weekly fast by picking the day of the week and the number of meals you want to skip. My suggestion is to consider fasting one entire day a week if you're newer to regular fasting. If you already have a good rhythm, look at fasting a day and a half or even two days a week. I started fasting one day a week in college without much equipping from others or experience in fasting, and it was doable, even with a full workload of school and work. Many people in my life have regularly fasted one day a week in every kind of life season, so I know it's doable and can be enjoyable for most people. Also, pray about joining the 3-day Global Bridegroom Fast that IHOP-KC hosts every month. Depending on your rhythm, joining in monthly or every few months could be very doable and impactful for you.

Be creative and strategic in how you schedule fasting times. Think through your week and pick the days and times that allow you to get as much time as possible with the Lord. Also, is there a day that works the best for you to have a little less energy? Do you have other weekly commitments you want to plan around, or can you move things around so that you have a whole day that has fewer commitments?

In my current life situation, I have a family with three young children that demand my energy in cooking, cleaning, feeding, and, most importantly, playtime! For me, creative scheduling looks like starting my fast after lunch on Mondays and ending at noon on Wednesdays. Beginning on Monday afternoon allows me to have enough energy to be with my family the rest of that day, and then Tuesday and Wednesday morning, I get extra prayer times. I eat a small lunch on Wednesday, and my energy levels increase to be fully present with my family the rest of the day after work. Because Tuesday is the only day that is potentially affected by my energy levels, we schedule easy meals for dinner that night and don't schedule hangouts to lighten the load of the evening.

If I need a nap or extra prayer time during dinner on Tuesdays, my wife gives me the freedom to do so. Otherwise, I spend that time with my family without eating. I've explained my reasons for fasting to my kids plenty of times in the past, but sometimes I remind them at dinner time. Now they understand it enough and hold me accountable if I start snacking on dinner!

FASTING TYPES

Research each of the four common types of fasting (water, liquid, partial/ Daniel, Benedict), and decide which one you want to try consistently. You can be creative with this as well and combine them in different ways. An example is if you want to fast for two days, but you're not ready to do a liquid fast. You could fast with juices on one day and then do a Daniel fast on the second day as a way of transitioning into two days for a while and see how that goes for you.

I have two suggestions for choosing fasting types. The first one is to try liquid fasting. If you think your body isn't healthy enough to handle it, talk to your doctor and get a plan for what will work for you. If you're healthy but overwhelmed by the idea of fasting on only liquids, talk to God about it and address your fears. Ultimately, do the type of fasting that you're ready for and excited for, but be aware that the fear of not having food might be exaggerated until you try fasting one day. The second suggestion is to stick with your plan for several weeks before altering the fast type or the length of fasting. Doing this will allow you to get a sense of how your body and heart acclimate and respond to how you're fasting.

CONSECRATION PLAN

To consecrate something means to make it sacred and set apart from ordinary life. How can you make your fasting time holy? In what ways can you make it different from the other days of the week?

VISION

This vision category includes a written vision statement, written down fasting times (precisely when you're starting and ending), and a short prayer list for fasting days. In your journal, write down your weekly vision and desires for fasting, along with any specific prayer topics you want to pray into each week. Your prayer list could include long-term prayers and short-term prayers that could change on different weeks. The basic questions you're answering in your vision statement and prayer list are, "Why am I fasting this day each week, and what am I asking for in prayer?"

When I look at my vision statement on fasting days, my heart is aligned with purpose and consecration, and I recognize the holiness of what I'm stepping into. This makes the fast more enjoyable, strengthening my resolve when I'm tempted to break my fast early.

The same thing is true when I pray through my short fasting prayer list. If I pray through it consistently over weeks, it becomes an instant source of life and connection to my fasting vision, and it increases my faith and resolve to keep fasting. If you pray them consistently through the fasting day, they become deep wells of life on future fasting days. This is especially true on a longer fast, but even on a 1-2 day fast, connecting to the vision and prayer points is powerful and necessary.

In the weak or mundane moments of fasting or the moments of subtle demonic discouragement, God will use your vision statement and prayer points to bring your heart back into alignment. Fasting is challenging by itself, but the demonic kingdom also wants to get you to believe your fasting doesn't matter so that you lose faith in the moment and break your fast. It's subtle, but it's real. If they can get you to believe that what you're doing isn't doing anything or isn't doing much in the spiritual realm, you'll be more tempted to give up.

EXTRA FEASTING TIME

When you're fasting from food, you are positioned to depend on, hunger for, and feast on the Lord's presence in a more tangible way. Deuteronomy 8 says we don't live on bread alone; but on every word that comes from God's mouth. This takes on an entirely new reality when you're literally not eating food to comfort or sustain yourself. In many ways, you will depend on experiencing God's presence and fellowshipping with Him, but it's more than just being "sustained" to get through the day. It's about having your spiritual longings satisfied in God in a unique and focused way. God wants to train your soul to "live" on His Word more than you live on food.

Fasting from food is feasting on God's presence. The goal on a fasting day isn't just to make it through the day by any means necessary. The goal is to feast on God with the extra time, space, and hunger. With this in mind, I suggest scheduling as much time with God as possible. You are going to have times of feeling tired, bored, and lazy. In those times, you're going to be tempted to fill or waste your time on things you're used to (YouTube, books, admin tasks, busyness, coffee hangouts) that don't directly connect you to Jesus. When we turn to these things, what we're really doing is distracting ourselves from physical hunger and spiritual boredom until we can eat food again. I have done this so many times, and it takes away from the true purpose of fasting.

Be creative and even stretch yourself to spend more time with Him than you think you can. Think outside the box of your regular schedule and find ways to get long chunks of time and even fifteen minutes at times throughout the day. Get some morning prayer, maybe an afternoon break, and then some time before bed. I didn't even know how to fast in college, but I spent hours in prayer outside of my classes and homework times. When I was single and working full-time, I prayed in the morning, prayed or napped during my lunch break, and spent the evening at my church prayer meeting. I've had friends in all kinds of family or workplace settings, and they've put the extra effort in to make fasting work. If a workday doesn't work for you, how about a weekend or a 24-hour slot from Friday until a Saturday lunch?

When you spend more time with Him, you'll experience His nearness and feast on His presence. That might sound crazy if you haven't done it before, but something in your soul will love the place of fasting if you consecrate your time to Him. How can you get more time in the morning, afternoon, and evening? How can you set your heart or arrange your atmosphere to engage with Him even while you're working or taking care of your kids?

SAYING NO

Consecrating your schedule to the Lord also means saying no to things that disrupt your fasting day. You have to decide for yourself what being flexible means, but my value is to say no ninety percent of the time to hangouts or responsibilities that would make me eat food on my fasting days or have less prayer time. Prioritizing fasting and prayer reflects your love and desire for God, so it's a holy thing to keep it!

FINISHING WELL

Set your heart to finish your fasts well without breaking early consistently. For most people, there's going to be tension between being too strict or too loose on finishing fasts. Growing in clarity and wisdom on how God feels about us breaking early versus us fulfilling our fasting commitment is a journey in Bible study and seeking the Lord's heart. As a starting point of discussion, I say try to finish your fasts as often as possible, even when it's a little challenging, or you feel like giving up. Yes, you're not proving anything to God by finishing, and He's ravished by our love no matter what, but I see lots of benefits to pushing through in the challenging moments and wrestling with beliefs in the process.

35

WEEKLY FASTING PART THREE

█ FASTING CHALLENGES

PHYSICAL CHALLENGES

There are at least three different physical challenges involved with fasting. The obvious one is lower energy levels. Depending on the type of fasting, you will have varying amounts of decreased energy. The point of fasting is to have less energy and enter into the spiritual principle of weakness that Paul and Jesus preached. While it's a real challenge to be aware of, it's to be embraced with the revelation that God's power will increase.

Set your heart to be okay with less energy and less productivity on fasting days. You can monitor your juice or vegetable intake to maintain a sustainable, though lower, energy level. Honestly, it doesn't have to be too bad, but you have to be aware of it and embrace it to whatever level you fast. Water-only fasts are very challenging because of the lack of energy, but juice and Daniel fasts are very sustainable. I've done short and long juice and Daniel fasts consistently and have found them to be very doable for people in all kinds of situations. Don't let the fear of unknown energy levels hold you back from growing in weekly fasting or more extended fasting.

The second challenge on a fasting day is experiencing detoxification symptoms. During fasting, the body naturally begins to rid the body of toxins or things that are unhealthy. When this happens, there are headaches, dry mouth, bad breath, joint pain, tiredness, acne, and increased mucus. Some of the physical discomforts are also related to your body going without specific daily intakes such as caffeine and refined sugars.

One fear people have about fasting is that they will experience detox symptoms every week. Don't let that be your fear! There are lifestyle changes you can make to address potential detoxing. I've found taking walks outside, stretching, and drinking healthy juices help with any detoxing that may be happening on fasting days.

The last physical challenge is to change your lifestyle to promote enjoyable fasting. You can research ways to help with the detoxification symptoms, but the longer-term solution is to evaluate your lifestyle and make changes that decrease your toxin intake. Yes, begin and end your weekly fasts with intentionality, but eating healthy and intentionally most days will make fasting even easier. Regular exercise will also cleanse and strengthen your body during the week. If you want to step into fasting, you will be faced with any unhealthy diet, exercise, and rhythms you have, so you might as well address some of them now.

My wife and I eat relatively healthy, and because of that, I don't experience the consistent detox symptoms I used to in my early days. We were radical and cut every source of refined sugar in our diet and recipes, and replaced them with honey, or stopped eating them altogether. During Bible school, I didn't eat healthily or drink healthy liquids on fasting days. I made fasting much harder than it needed to be! It is so much easier now that I'm eating healthier and transitioning in and out of fasts wisely, and the detox symptoms are usually only there if I ate badly the week before.

EMOTIONAL CHALLENGES

Emotional challenges include low emotional energy and unpacified emotions. I don't know the science behind this, but depending on how your body responds to fasting, you may have lower energy in your emotions. This is similar to having less physical energy.

Your emotions will be raw and unable to be pacified by everything that usually supports them. In my opinion, this is the most significant challenge of fasting! Think of all the things you might say no to on fasting days: movies, YouTube, social media, unintentional hangouts, books, drinking coffee, cooking, and eating food. Your emotions are stimulated, supported, or distracted by some of these things daily. These are probably the things you turn to when you feel sad, discouraged, bored, angry, confused, and overwhelmed. But on fasting days, they are all stripped away.

Emotional crutches are exposed in fasting. When this happens, the actual state of your heart will be revealed. In this place, you will hopefully see the areas of your heart where you are dull or broken in your relationship with the Lord. You might feel great and "connected" to God on Sundays when there's a coffee in your hand, loud music, and lunch right afterward. But how do you feel when there's no other stimulation, and it's just you, your Bible, and Jesus all day?

I don't fully know what your journey will be like, but the exposure of emotional crutches will be a good thing. Realizing that there are areas of dullness and brokenness in your heart is the first step towards hungering and thirsting for God to be our source. You can't be hungry and thirsty for God if you're filling your soul with other things, and you won't encounter God as much without cultivating spiritual hunger.

The process of realizing spiritual dullness, unto awakening spiritual hunger for God, unto a more focused pursuit of God, cannot be bypassed. Spiritual hunger is always the prerequisite for something more in God. Jesus said that those who hunger and thirst would be filled, and David said, "*O God, You are my God; early will I seek You; my soul thirsts for You; my flesh longs for You in a dry and thirsty land where there is no water. So I have looked for You in the sanctuary, to see Your power and Your glory.*"[1]

If you can say no to all the emotional band aids on fasting days, Jesus will heal them and become your source of life over time. Fasting and being stripped of all the crutches is the barren wilderness in which He wants to encounter you and transform your appetites. Just like the Israelites in the wilderness, God wants to remove all the emotional supports and train your soul to feast on Him alone.

RELATIONAL CHALLENGES

Relationship challenges sound like an odd difficulty, but they are real. King David and John the Baptist experienced challenges in their relationships because of fasting.[2] Fasting is a strange topic in itself, but it's a whole lot stranger to people when fasting is a part of your lifestyle. Some of your family, friends, co-workers, and church friends might not know what to do with the topic or understand how to interact with you on fasting days. This is where the challenges lie.

---

[1] Matthew 5:6; Psalm 63:1-3.

[2] Psalm 69:6-10; Matthew 11:18.

There are ways to keep fasting days private so others don't even know you're doing it, but some people will figure it out, and others you'll want to tell at necessary times. So, what happens when people know you fast regularly or that you're on a longer fast? Some will be intrigued and ask questions, which is amazing! Some won't be sure what they can ask you because fasting is mainly seen as a private thing. This will leave them unsure of what to say or how to interact with you on fasting days. You might be the only person they've met that actually fasts. Others might inwardly or verbally disagree with fasting, either for perceived health concerns or because of their Biblical perspectives. Another group of people might feel challenged, convicted, and provoked by your fasting and assume you think they should be fasting as well, even if you never call them to it.

What can you do in these different situations? My first response is that you don't have to tell everyone you're fasting, and you can fast in ways that keep it hidden from a lot of people. As you fast weekly, you will figure out ways to keep it hidden. If it's going to be evident to certain ones, come up with a short explanation of why you fast. Bring them into a dialogue to ask questions or share concerns and help them understand how they can relate to you on fasting days, like if they should invite you for a meal, break time, or workout session. The awkwardness and confusion can be removed by good conversation.

If you are intentionally telling your Jesus-loving friends, have a Biblical explanation and a heart reason for fasting, and be ready to respond in love to all kinds of positive or negative responses. If they are close friends, the conversations could be very healthy and help them understand your heart and get a vision for fasting in their lives.

SPIRITUAL CHALLENGES

The two spiritual challenges that I have observed are demonic resistance and the awareness of wrong motivations. Whether felt or not, there will be some level of demonic resistance in your life if you pursue fasting. Resistance could look like an increased accusation in your thoughts, greater temptation to break a fast, increased lusts or opportunities to express sin, negative situations, hard prayer times, relational conflict, and demonic dreams. On the other hand, God's power will increase in your life in every area if you pursue fasting, and His power will be greater than the Devil's, so there's nothing to fear. Be aware that fasting is a spiritual threat and recognize that some challenges might be demonic and will have to be overcome through prayer and diligence.

FASTING BENEFITS

In the first fasting chapter, I highlighted a few benefits related to intimacy with God: a longing for God, tenderness, and expanded heart size. Below is a list of four more spiritual benefits. We have to recognize and celebrate the benefits of fasting to build a personal testimony that will encourage us in the fasted lifestyle.

VULNERABILITY TO TRUTH

Fasting breaks down our defenses and makes us vulnerable so that God's truths can go deep in a quick way. If you compare the heart to the soil in a garden, then a fasting heart is soft, wet, fertilized soil compared to hard, dry, and malnourished soil. The fasting process is like pouring water on hard ground, breaking the soil into small pieces, and then mixing fertilizer into it until it's a perfect environment for seeds to enter and grow. The seeds of God's Word are then released into the soil and easily penetrate it and go deep. Then they bear much fruit! Fasting prepares the soil of our hearts to receive and nourish the seed of God's Word.

CLARITY

I liken the clarity that comes through fasting to someone getting their head above the clouds on a dreary day or to a blinding fog evaporating. In both cases, darkness or something was hindering clear sight, but in the process of fasting, the hindrances are removed to see clearly. I experience substantial clarity in thoughts and emotions in fasting, and I get a renewed vision for my life. Detoxing during a fast can hinder clarity, but if there is minimal detoxing, or if I'm 1-2 days into a short fast, my mind becomes more alert and able to think about the Lord. My emotions feel clear and more connected to truth, and I feel spiritual clarity and discernment in other areas of my life. Lies I have been believing become more apparent and easier to address in prayer. Sinful patterns are clearer to me and easier to turn from in confession and repentance. Accusations or any other oppression that I've been under become more apparent and easier to address.

These are a result of the complete silencing and stilling of the body and soul during fasting. Anxieties, fears, confusion, lusts, and physical appetites diminish, creating a unique quietness that makes everything clearer. God's whispers are easier to hear, and processing thoughts and emotions are significantly easier. Every time I experience this, I'm somewhat shocked by the quietness and the grace to process life in an organized way.

HEART POSTURED TOWARDS GOD

Our hearts are postured towards something or someone for satisfaction all the time. Fasting postures our hearts towards God for life through the day as opposed to other natural sources. On fasting days, I become more aware of the earthly things my heart is postured towards. When I'm aware of this, I can choose to turn or set my heart on God in the moment. Because of posturing my heart towards Him repeatedly during my prayer times, my heart begins to look to God more naturally throughout the week.

> *"So He humbled you, allowed you to hunger, and fed you with manna which you did not know nor did your fathers know, that He might make you know that man shall not live by bread alone, but man lives by every word that proceeds from the mouth of the LORD."*—Deuteronomy 8:3

In Deuteronomy 8, God brought Israel into the wilderness to change the orientation of their hearts from external and temporal to internal and eternal. The wilderness caused them to be aware of what they looked to for life through the day so that they could address it and turn to God for life. As we fast from food and other sources of life, God wants our hearts to learn that the intimate Words of His mouth are the real source of life. In this process, our hearts turn to God as the source of life, impacting the heart on non-fasting days. This process trains the soul to look to God through the day and transforms your internal appetites to desire God.

HEART AGREEMENT

The "yes and amen" in our hearts grows stronger and deeper as a result of fasting. Whether it be a 1-day fast or a 40-day fast, God strengthens our wills to agree with His values and commandments. We are supposed to agree and say yes to His values in everyday life, but there can be a resounding and sustained "yes" within fasting. This could pertain to His promises over our lives, His love for us, or conviction in an area of righteousness. In the tenderness of fasting, our hearts can dynamically grab onto the truth.

WRONG MOTIVATIONS?

Will you have wrong motivations in fasting, like losing a few pounds, impressing others, or trying to earn something from God? Yes, you probably will! You might not be aware of them right away, but they will likely come to the surface after more fasting. Are these your entire motivation for fasting? You'll have to ask the Lord about that, but there's a good chance you're fasting out of a sincere desire for God, and these other motivations are mixed in to different degrees.

I counsel people to respond to wrong motivations by repenting before the Lord, confessing to friends, and not quitting their fast. Why not quit the fast if the motives are not 100% pure? Because fasting is part of what positioned you to see your motivations clearer and fasting will be what positions you to receive breakthroughs from the wrong motivations. Compare wrong motivations in fasting with wrong motivations in prayer or Bible study. Would you stop praying or reading your Bible if you became aware of wrong motivations? No, prayer and the Word are the sources of deliverance and clarity.

Clarity is a sign of God's work of wisdom and revelation, so praise God you see clearly. If there are mixed motivations in fasting, the same mixed motivations are with every other spiritual activity. If this is true, God is probably addressing a root issue affecting your entire approach to relating to Him.

When you're aware of the wrong motivation, take a minute and talk to God about it and address it by repenting of it. God might encounter you with the truth if you tell him your motivations and talk it through with Him. As often as the motivation comes to the surface, repent of it and bring it up to your close friends for prayer and accountability.

In more extreme situations with body image struggles and eating disorders, you should stop fasting. If you or a friend struggle with either of these issues in fasting, bring them up to your trusted church leaders for counsel.

WHAT IF I BREAK EARLY?

How does God feel if you break a fast, and what should you do when it happens? He's deeply moved by our desire and attempts to fast. God's heart is easily overcome with love by the movements of our hearts towards Him. He sees the slightest movements of love and desire that get you to fast and spend time with Him, and it ravishes His heart![3] God is not discouraged or disappointed in you for breaking, and He's not calling it a sin. God is blessed by you, celebrates your attempt, and He sees where you're going in fasting in the long-term journey of it all. God is a proud Father over your life!

God isn't an angry father who has unrealistic expectations of His children, who isn't willing to go through the process of training them in something. He's gentle and patient, and He's with you in the journey of fasting, just like every other area of your life. God is a Father who leads you by inviting you into things, encouraging you, directing you, and then laboring with you for maturity and consistency. If you are newer to fasting or stepping out in new ways, God is holding your fingers through it like a father helping his child learn how to walk.

PUSH DELETE

When you break a fast early, you have the choice to jump back into your fast with a happy heart or to start up again the next week. I love what Mike Bickle always says, "Push delete and get back in." If you have the resolve in your heart to fast, jump back in with no shame or guilt before God! If you don't have the determination to fast, decide to end and get ready for next week's fasting time.

MATURING IN FASTING

I believe God wants us to be free from shame and guilt in breaking early, but He also wants us to mature and be able to persevere through tempting moments. If you notice you regularly break your fasts, re-evaluate your fasting commitment or talk to the Lord about why you're struggling. You have to walk free from shame in breaking early and carry the sobriety of wanting to sow in the Spirit in fasting and being diligent. At times, I've gotten into patterns of breaking early consistently, and I've found that I have to re-consecrate my fasting times to the Lord. When I make the shift in my heart to take it more seriously, I connect to the power of fasting, and I walk out fasting with more vision and diligence.

If you consider the sowing and reaping principle or the weakness principle, fulfilling your fast does matter. If you're consistently breaking early, you're going to miss out on

---

[3] Song of Songs 4:9.

some levels of the fasting benefits. It's the same with prayer; if you always spend less time in prayer, your heart will experience less.

If you are having a hard day with fasting, you can talk to the Lord about it and see what He says, but I don't think you have to ask His permission to break early. If you don't want to fast that day and don't have the resolve to ask Him for help and persevere, don't feel bad about breaking.

█ WEEKLY ASSIGNMENT

This week, reflect on any fasting days you've done during the module and refine and adjust your fasting plans as needed. For some of you, you might be ready to plan for more fasting, and for others, refining may only include small adjustments. Answer the same questions but write down more detailed thoughts if you have them. *Questions to answer: (1) What day/meal(s) will you fast? (2) What kind of fast will you do? (3) How long will it last? (4) When would you pray? (5) How will you prepare food-wise? (i.e., what will be your last meal, and what will you break your fast with?)* If you choose to fast according to your plan during this week, journal your thoughts, challenges, and experience from the fast. Reflecting on your fast will help your heart and help you refine your plans.

To end this program, schedule a 1-3-day fast with your group. Schedule how long it will be and what days are best. Then plan when the individual and group prayer times will be. I've led people that were newer in fasting into 1–3-day group fasts and it was a great experience for them, though stretching. These fasts started on a Friday morning and ended on a Sunday evening with group prayer times every morning and evening. A group fast is beneficial during this module because it helps bring the group into the next step of fasting with the grace that comes in doing things together. It also stretches people to taste long prayer hours three days in a row, which can tenderize hearts quickly and get people longing for longer hours moving forward.

DISCIPLESHIP MEETING GUIDE
MODULE 8: FASTING – CHAPTERS 34 & 35

MEETING FOCUS:

The purpose of this meeting is to continue to process the prayer assignment (fears, hindrances, and what excites you concerning fasting), process how fasting is going, and work on a weekly fasting plan.

DISCUSSION QUESTIONS (IN ORDER OF IMPORTANCE):

1. *Spiritual pursuits:*
   a. Practically, how is your prayer schedule going? How many days have you walked out your prayer schedule? Do you need to make small changes to your schedule? How are your daily prayer times going, and how is God impacting you through them?

2. *Chapter questions:*
   a. Chapter 34 – Discuss any journaled thoughts and questions from the chapter. What are the most helpful practical questions you have? What were your thoughts on the Consecration Plan section in the chapter?
   b. Discuss your finalized weekly fasting plan. If you're fasting, how is it going for you? Do you have more you need to process and pray through regarding fasting experiences, fears, hindrances, wrong motivations, or things that excite you about it?
   c. Chapter 35 – Discuss any journaled thoughts and questions from the chapter. Which fasting challenge and fasting benefit impacted you the most?
   d. Talk through what the 1-3-day fast could look like for you this week.

3. *Heart Issue:*
   a. Share how your heart issue has been going this past week. With heart issue discussions, process, confess, encourage, and pray together for God to release transformation. ***Pray in tongues together and ask God to release power to the heart issue.***

4. Briefly review next week's homework together.

MEETING NOTES:

_____

_____

_____

_____

_____

_____

_____

_____

_____

_____

_____

_____

_____

36

TRANSITION WEEK

▌CONGRATULATIONS!

Y ou did it! This is the last chapter of the discipleship program! I am so blessed by your diligence to stay in the place of prayer through all the challenges, circumstances, new topics, new rhythms, and allowing leaders and your church community to call you higher. ***This week marks 40 weeks of pursuing daily prayer.*** As you read this, I pray you have developed God's perspective on your pursuit over the 40 weeks and are encouraged by how much you've grown and how much you've sown that will be reaped in this next year.

▌CONTINUING YOUR RHYTHM

This last week is an important transition for you. You've had a lot of structure and support around you for 40 weeks, and now you must think about how life looks without the formal training experience and expectations of the program.

The goal of this program was for you to learn a lifestyle of prayer and have the support you need to grow into a rhythm of prayer. If you can transition well, you will maintain your new rhythms and values and continue to grow!

Your experiences with God in each module and the daily prayer rhythm you've grown in are priceless. In a prayer-less generation, what you've cultivated so far is a huge gift, not only for you but for those that you will disciple. Therefore, I strongly encourage you to steward your new prayer life by continuing in daily prayer and focusing on growing in each prayer expression. These 40 weeks have served to strengthen your foundation, but now you can keep building and grow upon it.

Deep daily intimacy with God through prayer is why you exist, and it's the only thing that will continue to satisfy and transform you. As I said in the beginning, the structure of this program is likened to the wooden forms and braces that keep wet cement in place until dry and in perfect shape. I'm confident that the cement of your prayer life has been formed and hardened in place, so now you can continue to build on your prayer life.

I realize that coming out of a structure with assignments and expectations it can be natural to "take a break" from such pursuit of God. Part of this is okay because you've been stretched, you've grown your rhythms, and you've had book reading and prayer assignments on top of normal life. So yes, take a couple of weeks off from assignments, but don't take a break from your prayer rhythm; that's where you're experiencing God's life. Satan would love nothing more than for you to stop or slow down in prayer for a month so that he can get you back into a spiritual rut.

TRANSITION OPTIONS

By design, most of the components of this curriculum can be continued within your local church long-term. There isn't a lot of mystery as to how you can continue growing in prayer with structure and community because everything you've been doing can be normal to continue within discipleship and your friendships at church. You don't have to grow in prayer alone! God has ordained strength for you through living in a church community. Below are the main components of the curriculum that can be continued.

MAIN COMPONENTS

1. **Daily Prayer** – You can continue your commitment of 1-2 hours of daily prayer. When you are ready, grow into longer prayer times each day.
2. **Spiritual Pursuits** – You can continue to fill out a new Spiritual Pursuits document every couple of months to maintain your spiritual clarity. This document was designed to be used long-term, and we use it as a part of our lifestyle. For every season of your life, this includes having Bible direction and plans, a heart issue to

pursue breakthrough in, and a part of your calling to grow in, as well as having a detailed weekly prayer schedule.

3. **Discipleship Mentor Meetings –** Within God's plans for the local church, it should be normal to be discipled and to disciple others. Therefore, God wants to encourage, strengthen, and challenge you by meeting   with a Discipleship Mentor regularly. We never have to graduate from being discipled! As a helpful guide, you could continue to center your conversations around your Spiritual Pursuits.

4. **Prayer Room –** If you started a prayer room or joined an existing one, keep it going each week. God designed you to grow in prayer and friendship with others by praying and reading the Bible together. Get a long-term vision for growing your prayer room and bring others into it so they can taste the glory of praying together. Investing time and energy into bringing people together will be worth it because God is worthy of more worship, and because prayer rooms are invaluable to discipling people in prayer.

5. **Learning Prayer Expressions –** When you're ready to focus on learning more about the prayer expressions from the curriculum, go through one module at a time at your own pace. You will glean more from each chapter the more times you go through them and apply the principles and practical tips. You could also go through other books that are focused on training people in meditation, tongues, worship, fasting, etc.

6. **Group Gatherings –** Within your local church, it should be normal to have Bible study groups or prayer accountability groups. You can continue to grow in your prayer life and share your life in God with others in regular gatherings. This could also include extended group prayer days on a regular basis.

STRUCTURE IDEAS

There are several relationship and structure options that you can transition into to walk out your prayer life. Each option provides the structure and support necessary to help you grow in prayer. If this is something you're desiring, consider which one or two options you would want to create or join if your church already has them operating.

1. **Prayer partners –** With this option, you could gather one or more peers to meet every one-two weeks to talk through your Spiritual Pursuits. In these times, you could share what God is doing in your times in prayer and the Word, confess sins

and testify related to your areas of transformation, discuss your desired areas of growth, pray for each other, and hold each other accountable to your Spiritual Pursuits. Also, you could focus on slowly reading one module at a time.

2. **Be discipled using the Spiritual Pursuits** – You could continue to meet with a Discipleship Mentor at your church with the Spiritual Pursuits topics as your main conversation. Within this option, there are lots of directions you could go based on what you want to focus on growing in (prayer expressions, dealing with heart issues, growing in aspects of your calling, or going through Bible teachings together).

3. **Disciple someone with the curriculum** – You could choose to disciple someone else through this same curriculum. Doing this would help you go through the content and assignments again to strengthen your rhythm. It would also cause you to grow in prayer and own the values more because you would be calling others into the lifestyle and modeling the way.

4. **Be discipled through the curriculum again** – If you feel the need to go through the entire content and structure of the curriculum again, I encourage you to do it. Your prayer life will be strengthened, your heart issues will be addressed more fully, and you'll glean more from the chapter contents every time you go through them.

WEEKLY ASSIGNMENT

For your last assignment, respond to the questions on the Transition Assignment document. This document will walk you through the practical questions you need to think through to transition well, so take your time so you feel clear about your next steps. Also, some of the questions are reflective of the last 40 weeks to help you see what God has done in you based on your initial Consecration Assignment responses from week one.

TRANSITION ASSIGNMENT
CONSECRATION ASSIGNMENT REFLECTIONS

1. Read through your Consecration Assignment answers from *Week One* of the program. To celebrate growth and victory, reflect on them, and write down which ones were answered by God to some measure.

2. Ask God the following questions and write down what you sense Him saying to you. How do You feel about my pursuit of You during this program? What did You do in my life and heart during these 40 weeks? What encouragements do You have for me as I end these 40 weeks?

3. Do you feel any measure of weariness from the structure and assignments of the program? How does the idea of continuing in daily prayer and group accountability (discipleship or prayer partners) sound to you? If you feel weary, take some time to ask God to wash you with His thoughts, and for Him to renew your desires and strengthen your heart from being stretched in your prayer rhythms and lifestyle.

PRACTICAL TRANSITION QUESTIONS

4. Ask God how He wants you to consecrate yourself to Him in this next season.

5. Which module impacted you the most and why? Which module topic would you like to study and grow in after the program?

6. What specific components of the curriculum do you want to continue using (refer to the "Main Components" section in the chapter reading)?

7. If any, what relationship structure would you like to participate in, and when would you want to begin (refer to the "Structure Ideas" section in the chapter reading)? Write down why you want that specific structure.

Write down action items of what you need to do and who you need to talk to based on your answers to questions 5, 6, and 7.

DISCIPLESHIP MEETING GUIDE
LAST MEETING: TRANSITION PLAN – CHAPTER 36

MEETING FOCUS:

The purpose of this week's meeting is to review your *Transition Assignment* and to decide how to transition out of the program well.

DISCUSSION QUESTIONS:

1. *Transition Assignment*
   a. Share what you wrote down for each of the questions in the Transition Assignment that were related to reflecting on your *Consecration Assignment* from Week 1.
   b. Share what you wrote down for each of the questions in the Transition Assignment about what next steps you want to take. Finalize a plan together.
   c. Take time to thank God for the past 40 weeks together, encourage one another, and pray over the next few weeks of transition.

MEETING NOTES:

_____

_____

_____

_____

_____

Thank You For Reading My Book! I pray it blessed you!

If this book was helpful to you, would you help me spread the word by leaving an
Amazon star rating or writing a brief review??

Ratings and reviews tell Amazon to spread the word, and they are the first thing potential readers look at when previewing a book.

Instructions:
1. Go to your Amazon account
2. look up the Going Deeper book
3. Click "Ratings" under the main title
4. Click "Write Customer Review"

About The Authors

We are lovers of Jesus who have been overwhelmed by God's goodness and beauty in prayer. We've walked through the normal obstacles that believers face when seeking greater intimacy with God and transformation and want to equip you to overcome your obstacles! We've been in full-time prayer and discipleship ministry since 2006, and currently minister at the Underground House of Prayer and Encounter Church in Sioux Falls, South Dakota. **Our 3 passions are**: multiplying disciples who take others deep in God's heart, raising up corporate prayer meetings and praying churches, and equipping parents to joyfully disciple their children in practical ways .

Prayer & Discipleship Resources

1. **Blog** (prayerdiscipleship.com/content/) - equipping topics on prayer, corporate prayer, intimacy with God, family, spiritual growth, godly friendships, and hearing God's voice
2. **Youtube** - view our personal content (**@prayer_discipleship**) or our church content (**@EncounterSiouxFalls**)

Upcoming Books & Video Courses

1. *Enjoyable Easy Prayer For Beginners: 12-Week Group Study Guide*
2. *Practical Guide to Hearing God's Voice: Beginners, Intermediate, and Advanced Courses*

Made in the USA
Las Vegas, NV
12 May 2024

89859913R00122